A Man
Without love

A Man Without Love

Cover design and artwork by Niven Dallas.

Front cover photo: The author hooking up the helicopter
load sling. Only ten minutes later the hook snapped, dropping the
almost new Mini Moke from 2500 feet into the desert.
Rear cover photo: A well-used Australian outback
gravel road, photo provided by Shutterstock.

Author website   www.nivendallas.com
First Published   November 2012
Paperback ISBN   978-0-9875833-3-8
E-Book ISBN   978-0-9875833-2-1

A Man
Without love

By Niven Dallas
Book three in the four book series
Dallas short stories

.

Authors Note:

This collection of short stories, are but a few reproduced from true events in the author's life. Be aware, the stories are not in any exact chronological order of events. However, I have attempted to set them in a sort of order, only to be reminded of an earlier tale too good to leave out.

These tales are carefully reproduced for readers, who appreciate interesting stories about people, at interesting times in the outback of Australia. Stories told from a new Australian's point of view, with a dash of humour.

The author has written these stories as close as can be remembered, drawing on the memories of those involved. Some of the characters names and the exact period, regretfully changed at the request of the persons involved. To avoid, well who would know what.

Nevertheless, these were great times. Providing a number of great stories, created by many memorable people and friends. Thank you all for allowing me to share these stories.

Table of Contents

Chapter One:	Accidents do happen	001
Chapter Two:	Trucking god rules	013
Chapter Three:	Dinner at the Sandfire Pub	025
Chapter Four:	Just a bit of bad luck	047
Chapter Five:	That was bad luck too	061
Chapter Six:	The flying Mini Moke	073
Chapter Seven:	I want a red Mini Moke	091
Chapter Eight:	French lead poison	105
Chapter Nine:	Australian Bastille Day	123
Chapter Ten:	Sacré bleu a two-piece Ute	135
Chapter Eleven:	Best effort to end it all	155
Chapter Twelve:	One can only try again	175
Chapter Thirteen:	A sign of our time	185
Chapter Fourteen:	Believe me I wasn't even trying	199
Chapter Fifteen:	Sorry I have lost your Toyota	209
Chapter Sixteen:	Keep trying until you succeed	233
Chapter Seventeen:	Monsoon Entertainment	261
Chapter Eighteen:	Love finally found	281
Introduction:	About the author	313

Dedication
Acknowledgements & thanks

This book is dedicated to Bill and the memory of his beloved wife Mary. In addition, to all the many people portrayed within these pages, including those who choose to remain anonymous.

For all the characters whose involvement in these stories who have made this book an interesting, funny, strange, frightening, and an educational read. Moreover, for all those who lead a full life... and can enjoy good laugh.

I must give special thanks to my very tolerant and understanding wife Lesley, who endured many years of a hermit husband... Writing is a lonely business.

Prologue

They say there are more than a thousand identifiable human emotions. In 2001 a bloke called Parrott identified and classified over one hundred prime and hundreds of secondary human emotions. Ekman in 1972 devised a list of some seventeen prime and many basic emotions.

Robert Plutchik's wheel of emotions in 1980 had it all figured out a bit different, suggesting eight primary emotions, expanding into many more secondary and related emotions... A bit confusing I hear you think.

Nevertheless, all of these esteemed experts do agree on some things, including in their primary emotion lists, six prime emotions that we humans apparently all experience. Love, Joy, Surprise, Anger: Sadness, and Fear.

Of these six human principle emotions, it would appear that the first emotion love is the most powerful and purest of all six. Love has a known close secondary connection to lust, longing, affection, and jealousy, continuing down the short list to finally the last prime emotion... fear.

Love as the first powerful prime emotion has a close connection with the other five emotions. A human being can experience Joy, and maybe a

Surprise, at finding love. Then again a person can experience Sadness, Anger, and Fear at the thought of losing, or… never finding love… a bit complicated eh.

By the way, this powerful emotion love is the basic subject that runs through all my connecting stories in this novel.

I have since discovered this love business is an exceedingly serious subject indeed. History has provided us with many examples of how love has influenced and changed a person's normal balanced state of mind. Wars bitterly fought, and Kingdoms given away, with many a murder committed in the name of love...

Yes I do fully understand that this is indeed a tricky subject for a simple business man like me to write about... but then again, I felt that I must write this particular moving true story while I still have most of the details in my mind.

Just whom do you turn to for guidance and advice on such a tricky subject as this… that's right, you're own loved one… the wife.

Problems surfaced early, especially after advising my lady that I was going to write a love story about one of our ex-employees, a motor mechanic named Bill Gump. My lovely wife Lesley delicately drove the enormous challenge and complexity of the proposed task home to me. Lesley demanded to know what qualifications I had to write about "Love," a subject she considered I knew absolutely nothing about... this was shattering news.

I gently tried to explain that this was a sort of bloke-love problem; being a powerful true love story. Not from a woman's point of view at all.

Lesley hoped that Bill and I would be very happy together and left me standing there with a confused look on my face, muttering under her breath and slamming the door behind her... Did I detect something wrong with my proposed book writing idea, or was it bewilderment at me taking a keen interest in another person's love-life, even though that person is... a bloke.

I do know for a fact that blokes really do experience the pangs of love a bit different from that of the ladies... It's all very difficult to understand, you see blokes don't ever talk about love and passion and all that sort of girly thing; no, they only talk about conquests. That is if you have ever been able to conquest anything; if not, well then you simply tell lies, and as time goes on... more lies, then the lies become bigger lies.

Mind you, at this same time in your early male/female attraction education of strange feelings, things just start falling into place. Your slightly more experienced macho male pals... You know the type, those cool guys with their shirt-tail hanging out, and displaying the start of what will soon become some face stubble; they will, with macho confidence casually drop a few hazy clues about things...

Now don't get me wrong, the healthy young Australian male is very much aware of these powerful mating desires, oh yes... Later on in life as a bar-bracing, beer swilling Aussie bloke, the heavy subject of love comes into the bar discussion quite often.

We blokes do talk about love all the bloody time; yes we do. For starters, all admit they have experienced the love of a sport, could be footy, or possibly horse racing, maybe we might love our job. On the other hand it could be a dream performance Ute, or car. Then we can also have a love of food, and drinking booze, possibly a good friend might deserve your love and respect, but be careful... no touching, or soft words. That sort of stuff could get you a swift punch in the face.

After a few years a bloke soon notices that his large group of pals down at the pub is getting smaller... then you realise why. The bastards are all caving in. They are all getting bloody married, and then you start thinking... is this it?

Slowly you figure things out, it's you, you are the problem... you are a slow starter. Too many years in love with motor cars, footy, and drinking, and having what you thought was a good time...

Now there is only the forty year-old pisspot budgie left propping-up the bar. The only one left out of a once large jovial crowd of pisspot drinking pals, and he hasn't talked any sense for years... and then it happens to you... Nature takes over; you feel the pangs of want for another... a sole mate... a woman.

There is not a more basic and more powerful human instinct that any normal red-blooded bloke has ever experienced, than that of the love of a woman.

Time slips by, months, then years, with many a good mating opportunity seemingly close, and now lost on a regular basis. What can a man do... the situation is not getting any better. Other important things just seem to happen in your loveless life to eventually thinking of yourself as a total failure in all that you loved... and once lusted for.

I will tell you the story of a young man who thought he would never find true love. Fortunately for him he was wrong, very wrong.

On the other hand, the long road to true love for this young man was rough and extremely painful... Might I add at this point, it was also a lot of hard work for those blokes who cared a bit about him, to help him succeed in his long search for... natural love.

Chapter: One.

Accidents can and do happen

The story starts in the year 1976, on a cold and rainy August winter's day in Perth Western Australia, if there is indeed ever a real winter in the City of Perth. Bill Gump had turned up for work at "Dave Johnson Motors" early as usual, always the first to arrive, and the last to leave.

This was a man who loved his job as a motor mechanic. Being not, just you're commonplace every day mechanic, but a fully indentured British Rolls Royce trained mechanic, a man who was used to working on... Proper motor cars.

With such esteemed qualifications, one would have thought to this man, working on lowly motor vehicles such as BMC Leyland and Datsun would have been a major comedown, presenting him with an image problem. Not so, this did not bother Bill Gump in the slightest, much the same as the winter weather outside that cold miserable wet day.

You see, the Perth winter weather was in Bill's mind much better, and by his experience, far milder than the English summer he had recently left behind in England. That's why Bill was wearing his normal everyday work outfit of steel capped boots, footy shorts, and tank-top while diligently working on a brand new motor car, a Triumph Pi sedan.

This beautiful car was just one week old, owned by a fussy local Doctor. The car reported to have an annoying and irritating engine flat-spot while accelerating hard from a standstill.

It was now seven-thirty in the morning, the workshop and sales people were just starting to arrive. They were all well wrapped-up against the bitter cold and lashing rain as they made a beeline straight for the coffee machine. As Peter stood in the coffee line, he glanced across at Bill and yelled out above the noise of the loud high-revving Triumph engine.

'Morning Bill, looks like you're going down the beach again later, I see you've still got some work to do on your new Aussie sun-tan.'

Then noticing the large bandage stuck with medi-tape to the left-hand-side of Bill's head, shouting above the engine racket again.

'How's your sore head this morning? It looks like the bump has gone down a little... that's always a good sign.'

Bill could not hear a sarcastic word Peter was saying because of the loud bellowing and revving of the Triumph engine.

Peter was Bill's best friend, possibly his only friend. Sadly, Bill was a bit of a loner who was always trying hard to fit in. Please don't get me wrong as Bill was a very nice bloke, and would do anything for you, and that was most probably one of his main problems. Some people would take advantage of Bill's very generous and helpful nature, and Bill unfortunately mistook this interest in him for real friendship.

The large bump on Bill's head was the result of a rather major motor car incident that had taken place only a week earlier. As we all know, motoring "incidents" can be otherwise described as... motoring "accidents." In this particular unfortunate incident, it almost cost Bill his life. The full details of which are most certainly worth mentioning at this early point.

Obviously Bill's interest was in motor sport, and he was just starting to get-known around town. After all, Bill had an extensive involvement in many motor sporting events when he was in England. On this occasion, one of the local rally sporting clubs (to which Bill was a keen member) was short of a rally mapping crew. Now these are the guys who plan and set-out the clubs future rally events. As such, each and every point and detail of the proposed rally route accurately measured and carefully written down. These details will eventually become the official rally-event competitor map, the final route plan.

Bill was thrilled when asked at short notice to take part in a new rally mapping lay-out when the normal map crew member caught a bad cold. The proposed new rally event, being planned, using an almost new Mitsubishi Lancer A73. This car is special and expensive, being very fast full-blown turbo kitted out rally car.

As the night unfolded, apparently in the beginning everything was going well, Bill complying with the strict club rules; as a result being firmly belted into the left front passenger seat with the standard full racing harness. Bill took this rally job very seriously indeed, knowing he was the responsible one who must enter down all the route details on the large note-pad strapped to his lap, assisted by the light of a small flexi torch.

It was around eight o'clock at night and dark as a dogs guts with no moon, when all of a sudden the proposed rally route took a sharp turn to the right. The Lancer driver then realising that he had just turned onto an unlit, un-controlled train level-crossing. The driver looked to his right to see the dark shape of a train, with no headlight speeding down the track towards them.

What happened next is still a little vague, as Bill has never quite recovered the full memory of those last few frightening seconds. However, it would appear by the conclusion of the Police investigation of the incident that the car driver suddenly panicked and ran from the Lancer... Leaving the car just a split-second before the freight train made impact. At the time Bill was so engrossed, head-down with his mapping and paperwork that he was unaware of the disaster that was just about to unfold... around him.

The large Diesel-electric freight train, ploughed into the right-hand-side of the Mitsubishi Lancer with such a force, that in an instant it crumpled the body to less than half of its original width. With screeching brakes, and a perfusion of bright flying sparks, the locomotive continued on down the line for a further eight hundred metres.

As the freight train began gradually slowing down, large pieces of the once new Lancer ripped off and thrown aside like discarded toys. This mangled horrifying sight all witnessed by the terrified train driver who eventually managed to bring the whole freight train to a full stop.

First at the accident scene was the badly shaken car driver, the owner of the once magnificent Lancer, who was convinced on seeing this wreck, that Bill was most certainly dead. Bill now covered in blood and very still. Nevertheless, the most terrifying sight was what remained of his almost new Mitsubishi Lancer rally car. The remains of the car now tightly wrapped around Bill Gump, who was still strapped into the front passenger seat, surrounded in a sort of tangled metal cocoon.

Immediately all hell let loose as this was a notorious rail crossing for such accidents. Ambulances, Police, and the Fire brigade arrived very quickly to the scene. Clearly for the attending emergency services it was just déjà-vu, as this same accident had happened at this same spot a number of times before.

Amazingly, the attending paramedics could find little if anything wrong with Bill, other than a few bleeding scratches. Although he did remain unconscious throughout the long two and half-hours it took the rescue team to cut him free from the car wreck using the "Jaws of Life."

Now this is an interesting, and powerful lifesaving gadget. It consists of a large set of hydraulic powered metal shears. They are so powerful they will quite easily chomp right through a car door frame and windscreen pillar at the same time in one mighty bite.

Apparently Bill was just regaining consciousness, as the rescue fireman started chomping through the tangled metal window frame next to Bill's head. Just then, the heavy shears suddenly moved, smacked hard by the sudden release of the springing newly cut metal, catapulting the heavy metal jaws hard into Bills forehead knocking him out cold again. When the emergency services were finished cutting Bill free from the Mitsubishi Lancer, there was all but nothing left of this almost new high performance rally car to salvage.

Bill woke-up a few hours later in hospital with a massive lump on the left side of his forehead, suffering a bad, bad, headache. He sat up, and immediately demanded to know what he was doing in hospital, stating that whatever had happened, it was not his fault. Bill was indeed right, it was not his fault. On the other hand being in the wrong place at the wrong time, (or should that be the right time?) coupled with more than the average person's share of bad luck, was to say the very least a plague on Bill's life to date. That bad luck was just about to visit Bills life yet again...

The noise in the small service workshop was increasing to deafening levels as Bill revved the Triumph engine to determine the car's engine flat spot. Now just about then, Ron the new car sales manager had arrived at work. He was also nursing a mighty sore head, though his headache caused by a different means. That being the abundant amount of booze he had consumed the night before at his friends bar-b-cue.

Clutching his cup of strong black coffee, Ron walked up to the side of the Triumph in which Bill was half sitting; his left foot working the accelerator pedal, and right foot on the floor. With Bill's position, the driver's door wide open, and as expected, the bonnet up. Ron yelled at Bill above the crescendo of engine noise, with voice and temper raised.

'Shut that fucking noise up you pommy asshole bastard, your killing off what's left of my surviving bleeding brain cells.'

Bill was not amused at this rude comment. As I said before, Bill was a nice sensitive guy, there was no need for Ron to speak to him like that, and especially since Ron himself was a British import... a pommy.

With a wicked grin Bill floored the Triumph's accelerator with his left foot, at the same time giving Ron the up-yours finger. As Bill's left hand went through the motion to display the standard finger gesture, he accidentally knocked the automatic Triumph into reverse gear. The result was...well instantaneous.

The brand new Triumph Pi shot backwards across the workshop floor, covering the seven metre distance to the back brick wall in a fraction of a second. This sudden reverse movement caused Bill to plant his boot hard-down on the accelerator. Speed and velocity had built up to the point that the vehicle easily smashed through the workshop double brick wall, into the cold, rainy, winter's day outside.

Unfortunately the engine bonnet still being up; and firmly hinged at the front on this particular car, also the driver's door being open wide. This configuration then made a nice job of bringing down what was left of the six metre high brickwork hanging perilously over the now gaping hole in the back of the service workshop.

Had the vehicle been travelling a little slower, all the heavy concrete bricks would have landed directly on the vehicles roof, crushing it, and also Bill, no doubt ending his life. Nevertheless, this was not to be. The excessive speed at which the vehicle was travelling just cleared the main brick and rubble down-pore, thereby avoiding this possible life-threatening situation.

Unfortunately for Bill, the very last large concrete block fell from the full height of six metres. Bounced down the side of the now large dust bellowing rubble stack, and went straight through the front windscreen striking Bill squarely on the head, knocking him out... again.

Was this just a bit more of Bill's bad luck... well let's talk about that for a moment. Consider this; assuming Bill was killed in this unfortunate incident (which by all accounts and by the extent of the damage done, he should have)... well then, that would have been just bad luck. But...but...hang on there, Bill only suffered a heavy blow to the head, on the right-hand side this time, so was that some sort of good luck. Then again, who would bloody know?

A few hours later Peter picked Bill up from the hospital, he was quite well-known there now. Bill was now wearing a second medi-taped bandage to the right-hand side of his forehead. This matching the already medi-taped bandage on the left of his head, also having a large swelling lump of about the same size. Bill was very lucky indeed. On seeing him, Peter could not resist the humourist comment.

'Hi Bill, you look like the devil who's just had his horns amputated.'

Bill looked on in pain, not fussed or concerned by this smart comment. The nice-looking nurse had already made a similar one earlier. Nevertheless he was now more than concerned that his best friend Peter had found these two near-death accidents as... funny. He had expected a little more sympathy and understanding from his friend at such a painful time.

On the way back from the hospital Bill discovered there was more bad news; Peter had taken this prime opportunity to make known his latest career move, revealing his master plan. On hearing the plan Bill was shocked and most upset, mainly because he was not included.

Peter told Bill that he had accepted a job as workshop manager from his new brother-in-law up-in the North-West. His sister Lesley had married a bloke (me) who owned a small vehicle hire fleet, and automotive service workshop business in Kununurra, a remote town in the far North-West of Western Australia. He told Bill that his resignation from Johnson Motors was already in, and he planned to drive up to the Kimberley region next week.

This was all sad and bad news for Bill. He had survived being run-over by a speeding train while helping set out a rally, now his rally club no longer wanted him as a club member. Then he had driven a new car right through a solid brick wall like "Superman" suffering only a lump on the head, the only thing was he had lost his much loved job in the process. Now he was about to lose his best friend... all in one month.

On top of all this, Bill had just taken delivery of a brand new, Aspen Green, V8 powered, Leyland P76 Targa Florio motor car. A new car that he was dearly waiting for... but now being unemployed, he could no longer afford or find the monthly higher-purchase payments for. Then Bill had a brilliant idea. Turning to Peter, with what one could only described as a real devilish grin, he said.

'Pete, I've just had a pretty rough month; I think I bloody deserve a holiday to get over all what's happened to me. Two or three week's holiday in the Kimberly might be just what I need at this time.'

There was a low groan from Peter, and then quick-as-flash he replied.

'Ron the car sales manager was going to drive me up there in his new Datsun 180B sports XXX, Bill you know how small a car they are...'

Before Peter could finish Bill already had an answer.

'I'm only going for a few week's holiday Pete, I was thinking of driving up in my new Leyland P76; sort of give it a good run.' Then added, 'You can come along with me if you like, it'll save that bastard Ron getting his shitty little Datsun dirty.'

Peter was stunned into silence. He didn't want to upset his friend Bill by turning down his generous offer, although moved by another pressing reason; he most certainly didn't want to drive 3400 kilometres in the same car as Bill. Things just seemed to happen to Bill and motor cars, the cogs of fear were turning rapidly in his head, when Peter formed what he thought was a convincing answer to this tight spot...

'Ron has taken three weeks off work for a driving holiday, it's all been planned, and we're set to leave a week next Friday. I can't tell him at this late stage that I won't be going with him; it wouldn't be fair. He's been working on getting a few weeks away from his nagging missus for months now. It would ruin his plans for some peace and quiet.' Then as an afterthought Peter brightly added. 'Ron thinks this holiday break might even save his marriage.'

Bill was quick to snap back.

'What, me ruin his plans; hell Pete, that bastard Ron has just ruined my bloody working life, and cost me my job. You've seen what happened with that workshop accident; it was all because of him that the doc's car went through the bleeding workshop wall… I was nearly killed.'

There was an uneasy pause as Bill summed up all of the available options, concluding he only had one.

'All right then Pete; I'll just tag along behind you again. I'll follow you guys up to the Kimberley a week on Friday… I might as well, since there's fuck-all happening for me down here in Perth.'

Peter looked at Bill in utter astonishment. Not for Bill's unmovable decision to follow him up to the Kimberley, but for the positive statement Bill had made that nothing was happening to him here in Perth…

Therefore, it was reluctantly agreed, Bill would follow Peter and Ron up to the Kimberley on a driving adventure… What an understatement.

Chapter: Two.

Trucking good rules

When the Friday arrived, both cars set off from Perth for the Kimberley. It was a much later departure than was originally planned, and at different times, with Bill starting out a little ahead, with Peter and Ron following in close pursuit. Bill had no idea he was in front. This did not matter at this stage as the plan was for them to all meet-up at the Pier Hotel in Port Hedland; they had estimated this would be by sometime on Sunday.

In standard factory form the Leyland P76 Targa Florio could eat the Datsun 180B sports XXX in all areas of performance. Bill knew this fact, just the same as he also knew the Leyland P76 is the finest, and only five place passenger vehicle ever to be totally conceived designed, and built in Australia.

The P76 in terms of motor-vehicle design was leap-years ahead of the other so-called Australian built vehicles of the time. Those existing vehicles being the American owned General Motors Holden, the Ford Motor Company car, and the soon to be dumped Chrysler Valiant. All of which were just old, out of production American vehicles; superseded compact or town cars, then rebadged as Holden's, toughened-up a bit for our poor Australian roads.

This all new Leyland P76 was such a threat to the American owned Australian motor vehicle industry, to which the Prime minister of the day; the one-and-only hard-core socialist Gough Whitlam was moved to act. This man openly called this car "a dud," stating, "we have four Australian car manufacturers; and there is only room for three." The automotive industry unions had little doubt in identifying which car the Australian Prime Minister was talking about that must go. They then went about a sinister plan to destabilise and halting the manufacture of this all Australian designed and engineered dream car.

With the help of the socialist AMWU (Australian Manufacturing Workers Union) and a well construed pack of bureaucratic lies fed to a willing Australian media... he succeeded, and over 5000 Australian Leyland workers lost their jobs. Leyland Australia capitulated under the relentless union assault, closing down their Australian manufacturing of all vehicles in Australia and went home to the United Kingdom, vowing never to ever return... Australia's own designed, engineered and built car was gone.

Bill knew he had no real competition, as such; this trip should not turn into a race of any sort. He would do what he had agreed to do, and that was to tag along, following them up to the Kimberley. It was late August 1976; it was also a leap year... if that may have any bearing, or add some special depth and meaning to this story... well you never know, other things have…

As I said, departure day started out a bit slow as all concerned had been celebrating and partying like mad until the early hours. Both cars got underway late in the morning from two different locations. Perth to Carnarvon is 903 kilometres of good sealed road, taking Bill about eight hours of solid driving. It was just about this time that Bill had to consider some sleep, a very cautious judgment, caused by the near head-on collision from an oncoming road-train cattle truck.

Bill wisely decided to call it a day and pulled over to sleep in a "Truckie stop" (a sort of large road siding purpose-built for truck-drivers to pull-over for a compulsory rest.)

Bill was about 100 kilometres north of Carnarvon, and no doubt sound asleep when the Datsun 180B sports roared past on the dark road. The boys had decided to take turns, and drive non-stop right through to Port Hedland, a total distance of 1775 kilometres.

On the other hand Bill was about to experience some other confusing car problems. He was still sound-asleep when the two large road-trains pulled into the truck stop, the drivers deciding to teach him some basic trucker's rules.

Sometime later Bill then vaulted into the world of the living by a sudden need to have an urgent piss. In the dim light of the moon he noticed a large piece of cardboard that somebody had placed behind his steering wheel, reading the thick black texture words with the help of a lit match...

"Don't wake us up if you want to keep your front teeth, and you're cooking the bloody breakfast."

Bill thought how odd, as he got out of his car to attend the call of nature. It was just about then he noticed that his Leyland P76 was firmly wedged in-between two huge transport trucks. At his rear was a massive towering bull-bar on the front of a Mack Thermodine truck, and in front the last freight trailer of a huge road-train. Both vehicles were so close, they were all but touching his beautiful new Aspin green Leyland P76.

Bill was fuming mad, and in the dark strutted up to the front truck. Looking up at the cab Bill could just make-out two well-worn boots sticking out of the window and hearing the loud snoring of the driver. He had clenched his fist and was about to bang on the side of the cab, then hesitated, again reading the sign he was holding.

"Don't wake us up if you want to keep your front teeth."

Just then, he heard a muffled sniff at his feet. Looking down in the dim light, he could clearly see a very large Doberman with white bared teeth staring up at him menacingly. The dog was not tied-up, it did not move, nor make another sound.

Bill slowly backed away from the truck, and the dog settled down lowering its head. Sitting back in his car Bill thought even the bloody dog was afraid to wake-up the truck driver, and so he wisely decided to wait... dozing off into a peaceful deep slumber.

About an hour later the rear truck driver blew his powerful Alpine air horns. Then yelled out to Bill to wake-up and crank-up the bar-b-cue for breakfast, as they wanted to get back on the road soon.

The air-horn blast took Bill by complete surprise, the noise causing him to jump bolt upright in his seat, hitting his tender head on the hard metal roof. This day was not starting out well.

Looking around Bill then noticed the big steel plate mounted on four steel tube legs, almost opposite to where his car was, well... wedged.

Firewood had been stacked neatly to one side and Bill soon had the Bar-b-cue going, turning to the truck driver who by now was out of his cab having a morning piss against the front-wheel. Bill decided that his front teeth were safe for now, as this big truck driver's alpine horn must awaken everything for miles around. He was still fuming mad, blurting out in frustration.

'Why the fuck did you guys block me in last night? I've got to get going right now, and anyway I don't have any food to cook.'

By then the second driver was making his way over to the bar-b-cue. Both truckies were huge men dressed in dirty blue singlets and shorts, shod with heavy steel capped boots. Both had an esky cooler in one hand and a fold-up-chair in the other. Settling down in their chairs in front of the Bar-b-cue, one driver handed Bill a bottle of olive oil and a bottle of beer. Bills eyes lit-up, thinking his luck had changed.

'The names Bert,' and then cocking his head in the direction, 'and this is Sam, just chuck the olive oil on the barbie then wash-off the hotplate with the beer mate. Drink only what's left... got it?'

They all shook hands, and then both started to drink their beers staring at Bill, eyeing him up and down in silence, inspecting his now seeping blood bandaged head. Bill felt compelled to say something...

'My names Bill, I'm on my way to Kununurra for a holiday, and this,' pointing to his bloodied head wounds, 'I had a little accident a few weeks ago and...'

Just then Sam raised his hand in a gesture of silence, lifted one large arse cheek off the chair, and let go a tremendous fart. Bill was not amused at this show of crude behaviour, or their disinterest in his painful accidents. Then looking at both truckies their faces were blank and expressionless at this flatulent event. Bert then opened his esky and handed Bill a plastic bag full of prime beef scotch fillet, six large steaks, Bill's mouth was watering, was this just a dream?

'Chuck e'm all on Bill, Sam's got some bacon, six eggs, and some curry leftovers from last night; but then you've just heard, and smelt all about that.'

Bill let out a chuckle at this joke, but the truckies just stared at him in blank silence, clearly not at all moved by this joke, if indeed it was a joke. Sam handed Bill another beer as most of his went on the hotplate, then caught by surprise Sam spoke for the first time, from his mouth that is.

'Ya-know, if you carry-on driving the way you do, stuffing-up and obstructing every bloody truck stop along the road. I know one thing for sure, you're not gonna make it to Kununurra alive mate.'

Bill cringed at the truckies blunt comment visibly shaken, his face must have conveyed his next question, and what did he do that was so wrong? Sam must have used-up his daily verbal allowance as Bert provided the educational response.

'Let me tell you something mate, trucks are king-of-the-road in these parts. The government didn't make these bloody roads for you shitty tourist blokes. No matey, they made them to get freight and live-stock up around the North-West... in bloody great trucks, got it.

To stay alive on these roads, all you gotta do is have some respect for the truckie that brings the booze and materials what's needed to survive in these here parts.

Always stay clear by parking on the inside of a truckie stop. So as to let all trucks pass through freely at any time, day or night... got it. Always move off the road to allow an oncoming truck a clear road ahead.

A road-train need's all of the bloody road width, most times both lanes. If just one set of wheels, or the last trailer were to go off onto the soft verge. Then the whole bloody million dollars' worth of truck and freight would be gone in a blink-of-an-eye. The truckie knows this shit could happen, and he won't bloody move, so you must, or suffer what's coming… a head-on crash. Remember this mate, these 'ear trucks are bloody built to handle a head-on crash so you can guess who will come off worst… got it.

Bill was remembering all right, he was remembering about last night's truck near miss. In his drowsy sleepless bad mood he was playing chicken with a truckie, trying to force him to move over. Bill at the last second was the one who chickened out, this being one of his smartest decisions made in a long time. He was still shuddering at the thought of what could have been, when Bert added.

'Another thing mate, always wait until a truck driver waves you to overtake him. He knows you're bloody-well there, would have seen you miles away so watch him in his truck mirrors for hand signals. He will flash three right indicator signals and wave you on if it's safe. Or if your bloody dumb and thinking of suicide he'll rapidly flash left and hold a hand up stop, don't you bloody overtake… got it.'

Bill was listening to all this information, while tucking in to a mighty good breakfast washed down with a couple of cold beers. He thanked the truckies for the food and drinks.

Then out of curiosity and last night's near-miss Bill asked Bert and Sam if they had ever had a bad road accident? Sam in grim silence, heaved himself out of his chair, folded it, and picked up his esky. Then turned and waddled across to his road-train rig, driving it forward a few metres to let Bill out, leaving Bert to answer Bills question.

'Sam's had two road deaths, one asleep head-on, and one drunken rear-ender-shunt while he was parked. I've had two drunks and a sound-asleep, all head-on. You can tell after a while driving that the vehicle coming towards you is weird, you flash them and blow the horns, but they still come on at full chat. One time I had even stopped my rig in the middle-of-the-road to reduce the impact. I was flashing the lights and blowing the horn right up to the impact.

Bill felt another shudder go up his spine. For the first time in his life he was feeling deep down another man's pain, Bert looked away to hide what a tough man always hides and said sadly.

'I had nowhere to go mate. I was pulling five trailers, a load of almost 200 tonnes. We have near misses almost every day on these roads so for Christs sake you bloody pass on the truckie rules to all your mates, it can save a life.' Then quickly picking up some briefly lost Aussie-male tough-truckie image, Bert ended with... 'got it.'

Bill was starting to understand why these guys didn't laugh much. They had a serious job, and then he thought about his own driving near misses, including

21

the one last night and shivered again at the possible outcome.

As Bill was driving out alongside the truckies, who were now carefully checking their truck loads, he asked his last question. One that was praying a bit on his mind...

'Bert, what would you have bloody-well done if I had woken you blokes up last night?

Bert said 'I'll let Sam tell you all about that one mate.' Sam took a shallow drag on his newly rolled cigarette, spat out a bit of annoying tobacco, and then in a matter-of-fact way replied.

'My dog Twinkles here knows it will get a bloody good belt around the head if it ever wakes me up. So while me dog Twinkles here was chewing you up, I would have cranked up the diesel and backed over your little bloody green car mate. Then Bert here would have smacked you in the mouth, just as he promised in his note, then I suppose we would have had to cook our own bloody breakfast eh.'

Bill was wide-eyed and astounded at this ruthless don't-give-a-damn response, then gently drove out on to the main Great Northern Highway. He was thinking how lucky he was not to have disturbed their sleep, and then again, there was the very nice breakfast he had for free. Now you would have to agree, that was what you would call real good luck.

The Carnarvon truck-stop to Port Hedland road was a quiet 780 kilometre drive on the newly finished dual sealed road, an easy six hours driving for Bill averaging around 130 kilometres an hour. Getting around the large road-trains was what slowed Bill up the most, but then again, Bill got plenty of experience in testing out his new-found truckie road rules.

The Port Hedland to Halls Creek section would be a different story, as all the roads from this point on, were unmarked being just single rough corrugated gravel. Most small rivers and creeks that crossed the road were just two wheel tracks of broken concrete, many were just large dip's in the gravel road, with a rusty hard-to-read name sign. Just about everybody drove along at around 70 to 80 miles per hour to beat the gravel road corrugations, producing huge clouds of gravel dust.

The only prior warning of a creek-bed was the faded name and flood level sight-pole, that's if you were quick enough to notice them. Hitting a creek-bed at eighty miles per hour was a memorable occasion... if you survived. The only advantage was there was little other road traffic to worry about. So colliding with another damaged vehicle stalled in the dusty creek-bed was rare, but it did happen. The disadvantage was if you needed help... it was a long-time coming.

The last of the sealed roads would finish just before the Goldsworthy turn off, so the arranged meeting at the Pier Hotel in Port Hedland was most important.

When Bill arrived in Port Hedland around 1pm on the Sunday, Peter and Ron were out sightseeing, they had arrived around 1am in the morning, a full twelve hours ago. Bill left a message at the reception, and then retired to the main workers bar for a hamburger and a few beers, and maybe a few rums.

At around 1:45pm Peter and Ron rocked into the bar and ordered a round of drinks, Peter caught sight of Bill sitting in the corner of the bar all alone and yelled out to him.

'Hi there Bill you made-it, come and join us for a drink.'

The look on Bill's face told Ron he should say nothing and shut-up, so he just picked up his beer and stared at the wall. Then with a sad look Bill related his story of the truckie stop to Peter, and how his head got yet another very painful bash. Noting the grim undertone Peter diplomatically changed the subject.

'I think we should all get going within the next half-hour, we could be having a cold beer in Fitzroy Crossing by about eight tonight.'

This bright suggestion did nothing to stimulate Bill into a cheery mode. Bill had already decided that today will be designated yet another miserable day.

'You guys go on ahead; I'll easily catch you up in that crappy Datsun. I'm going to stay and have a few more drinks... go on ahead, I'll be all right.'

Chapter: Three.

Dinner at the Sandfire Pub

Peter and Ron liked to set a fast pace on the road as they both enjoyed driving fast. Then again so did Bill. His love of driving was only second to his love of eating and drinking.

Bill's stay at the Hedland pub was a little longer than planned. The small crowd of people admiring his new Leyland P76, parked outside the pub, further delayed his departure. One large well suntanned bloke, with a self-rolled fag dripping from the corner of his mouth wanted to know all about this new flash car...

'What make o car is this mate, and ow fast does she go?'

Bill puffed out his chest and proudly answered the outback fine-car enthusiast, who was staring in awe at the large Leyland boot badge.

'This is the top-of-the-range Leyland Targa Florio; I've fitted the carbie with bigger jets and had her up to

180 so far, just out of Carnarvon. On the next long straight I hope to top 200.'

The large Aussie admirer was still staring at the Leyland badge while he rumbled out his advice.

'That'll be the Sandfire flats, a bit over arf a carton from here mate.'

Bill still had language problems in his new country, having only been in Australia ten months. He thought he was doing all right using "carbie" Australian for carburettor and "mate" every now and again, but some people, and some words, were just too hard for him to understand.

The further north he travelled, the harder it was for him to understand the locals... What language would they speak when he got all the way up to Kununurra...? Bill tried to engage this big Aussie in his native Australian lingo…

'It will need to be a good long and stretch of road to really try her out...mate. And what's with the "half a carton" stuff about... err mate?'

The big Aussie admirer looked down at Bill in a frown of disbelief. Then flashed a gummy smile of missing teeth, no doubt lost in some distant bar-room brawl; threw his head back, drinking his beer-can dry. He then crushed the can to a neat disc between the palms of his massive hands and gently popped the can-disc into Bill's top-shirt pocket.

'Twelve of them cept full is arf a beer carton mate. By the time you finish arf a carton you'll be at the Sandfire flats. Then you got eighty bloody miles of flat road in front of yer... That'll be a good place to try her out mate.'

As the big Aussie strolled away, Bill clearly heard him say, "I don't think you' gonna get 200 miles-per-hour out of that bloody car. Christ, even a Holden don't go that fast mate."

Bill jumped into his P76 thinking what was that guy on about; Australia was in kilometres not miles per hour... Maybe it's only in the cities, and the bush is still in miles per hour?

A quick glance at the clock startled Bill. He would have to get going now to arrive at Fitzroy Crossing at around the same time as Peter. To catch them up he would need to drive like a bat-out-of-hell.

Bill didn't have half a carton beer so he would just have to judge the distance to Sandfire flats with half a bottle of rum... Finally he was on the road again.

Peter and Ron were having great fun driving flat-out on the gravel road reminding them of country rallies around Perth.

After a few close shaves with death on the unfenced road avoiding Kangaroos, Emus, and cattle the fun was rapidly losing its nerve-wrecking thrill. Ron being older and wiser suggested that they should slow down a bit and let Bill do a bit of high-speed catch-up along an area known as "Sandfire Flats."

As the name suggests, the road is very flat, and very straight, it is part of the Great Northern Highway (although one would ask in those days what was "Great" about it?) Between Port Hedland and Broome, is a distance of some 630 kilometres of rough gravel unfenced road.

Around halfway along this road is the Sandfire Roadhouse. This is the only place you can refuel and get something to eat and drink before attempting the long road to Broome. Peter thought this would be a great place for both vehicles to meet up again.

Concerned that Bill might miss this important refuelling stop and just drive past the Sandfire Roadhouse turn-off. He had pulled up about two hundred metres before the roadhouse turn-off on the main highway, if you could call it a highway.

The idea of stopping on the side of the road was to make sure that Bill knew that they were about to head into the Sandfire Roadhouse. This brilliant Peter idea was in an attempt to flag Bill down well before the Sandfire turn-off.

There was another and most important reason to contact Bill; that was, if you missed the Sandfire Roadhouse, the chances were that you would run out of fuel well before Broome. That was depending on how much extra fuel you were supposed to be carrying. Peter had guessed right, Bill was carrying no extra fuel.

It was around five o'clock in the afternoon, at that time of the year the sun sets at just after five in the North West.

The shadows were already long with the sun rapidly setting behind Bill's fast approaching Leyland P76, now seen as a large billowing cloud of approaching gravel dust on the horizon.

This part of the Great Northern Highway is long, lonely, and boring; with not much traffic. You could drive for over two hours and not see another human soul, or any other vehicles. Bill's P76 could easily maintain 160 kilometres an hour, even on these gravel roads. Then again, this was the very place the guy in the Hedland pub said was a straight road for eighty miles... So why not; the road ahead was clear... To ease some of the boredom he would try driving his new P76 flat out.

The P76 was fast, a speed later claimed by Bill to be just under than 200 kilometres an hour... not a bad performance for what most Australians considered as just a large family sedan.

Well it was one of those boring times as Bill thundered down the middle of the gravel road. (Always best to stay in the middle-of-the-road, being the top of any crown. This also this gives you the best chance to correct a drift problem... should any such problems occur.)

Another very good reason why most experienced remote area driver's travel fast on gravel roads, is all to do with the road surface. Rough gravel roads quickly become corrugated with constant use. The true cause of dirt road corrugations is still a deep, and extremely misunderstood scientific mystery.

Then again, not many scientists drive for weeks at a time on gravel roads, teeth chattering and back aching to form a very useful scientific conclusion. Instead, they have however come up with a workable solution and total fix to this corrugation anomaly. Top and seal all of the problem roads with bitumen. Not a bad idea... and you have to admit, very original.

One thing that stumps most corrugation theories is that the corrugations always extend the full width of the road, not just where the vehicle tracks are. After many years travelling on corrugated roads I have formed my own Dallas corrugation theory.

I claim that the suspension and shock absorbers on all vehicles, trucks, and cars set-up a patter-frequency-pattern with their wheels over the loose gravel. The frequency vibrations extend sideways (at right angles) away from the wheels with the constant hammering.

Add to this the normal driver's attitude of attempting to find the smoothest or lowest corrugation surface. Then the best, or least corrugated part of the road area soon becomes the same as the worst.

One final act of nature completes the mystery, the wind; a condition known as the sand-dune, wind-drift effect... peaking, and toughing. A similar effect is also caused by seashore waves on sand.

If you travel on remote area roads, then you can't avoid corrugated out-back roads, but you can greatly reduce the bone shaking jolts and vehicle damage, by simply driving faster over the corrugated road surface. Apart from saving your vehicle suspension and tyres, not to mention your back, this also supports my corrugated road theory. Most drivers travel on dirt roads at a sensible speed of around 60-80 kilometres an hour.

I, along with many other outback road users, have discovered that if you double your road speed, to say 120-140 kilometres an hour. You then change the frequency from the bottom, or trough of the corrugation to the peak of the corrugations. In frightening words, skipping across the top of all the corrugations.

The result is really quite remarkable. There are however some major problems with this type of driving. You must understand that road tyre traction is greatly reduced, thus requiring your maximum full-time concentration to keep the vehicle under control, and on track. Bill, Peter, and Ron were experienced rally drivers, this type of dirt road driving was quite normal for them, and that's why they were all enjoying this fast drive up-to the Kimberley.

Peter noticed the large dust trail long before he could make out the vehicle, or for that matter could hear the engine noise. He just knew it was Bill by the speed of the approaching vehicle.

Stepping into the middle of the gravel road, Peter started to wave his arms about to catch Bill's attention... big mistake... real big mistake.

As the Leyland P76 came into full view, Peter could now make out Bill at the wheel. He was looking right at him through the windscreen, with a half-smile on his face, a smile that Peter mistook for some sort of recognition.

Peter not only misjudged the look on Bill's face, but also the incredible speed of the oncoming car. With barely a half second to spare Peter threw himself to one side, and was blasted the rest of the way off the road by the air pressure of the passing high-speed vehicle.

Picking himself up in a cloud of gravel dust, Peter staggered back to Ron waiting in the Datsun 180B Sport.

'Did you see that? That fucking shithead just tried to bloody kill me, he drove straight at me, didn't even blink an eye.'

Ron thought the whole episode as rather funny, and was laughing as Peter spluttered and coughed in the billowing clouds of dry gravel dust.

'C'mon Peter; only an absolute idiot would stand in the middle of an out-back gravel road trying to flag down a car, especially one driven by Bill Gump.'

Ron then winding up the Datsun window in an attempt to reduce the intake of billowing dust. Peter then opened wide the passenger door, filling the car with red gravel dust, and climbed in alongside announcing in a shaky dry voice…

'I need a drink to wash down all this road dust, and to celebrate my good luck, surviving a murder attempt by my good friend Bill. Let's head across to the Sandfire Roadhouse.'

Ron had lapsed into a deep in thought so Peter poked him with his finger, which brought him back to life…

'You know Pete, I was just thinking, if Bill had hit you I doubt that he would have even stopped. Not unless you damaged his radiator or something; and by then, he would most likely have been miles up the road.

By my reckoning Bill was doing over a hundred miles an hour (Ron was still old school; everything was still in the old mile measurements.) I don't think there would have been much left of you to send back home to your Mum.'

While Peter was pondering the vision of this last grim statement, Ron gently drove across the road to the Sandfire Roadhouse.

Well, this was a bit of an eye-opener for Pete and Ron. The bat-wing door's on the entry to the bar was the first notable difference. Ron burst through the door's bringing his hands up, fingers pointing like pistols, with Pete blundering through behind him.

All the noise in the bar abruptly stopped, and the many drinkers turned on their bar-stools to see who it was acting like a bloody idiot.

Pete and Ron froze at the entry, and took in the strange scene. The floor made from large flat rocks that looked well laid, although covered in cigarette butts.

The bar and all the liquor display cabinet shelves being all built in rough timber, made from various sorts of scrap wood. Being mostly old stacking pallets, railway sleepers, and packing crates, but well put together to form a very interesting sort of look.

What caught Ron's eye was an odd collection of faded business cards from all over Australia, and the world, displayed by rusty thumb tacks.

The cards were stuck to various parts of the timber fit-out, some displays totally covering the timber roof beams. Other areas had paper money from different parts of the world stuck to the walls in much the same manner.

One wall was covered in a display of various headgear firmly nailed to the wall. They ranged from sweaty, well-worn, cattle ringer's Akubras hats, to mining company hard-hats, and one lonely British world-war-two steel helmet with what looked like a bullet hole in the front. They all had some sort of name-tag or wording crudely scrawled alongside them. "Powder-monkey Irish Jack, blown into heaven by a careless fag, but we still have his hat."

The annoyed eyes stared back. Some blackfellas and some whitefella, some old Aboriginal Gins, and some pretty rough looking Jill-a-roos. Nobody was amused at this display of cowboy gun slinging through the bat-wing doors, as they had all seen it done too many times before.

In the corner of the bar stood an old blackfella ringer cowpoke, complete with salt rimmed sweaty Akubra hat to his dirty checked shirt, and moleskin pants. His whole bush-man image was perfect, being nicely finished off with a pair of well-worn RM Williams riding boots.

The hand-rolled cigarette wobbled up-and-down in the old ringer's mouth indicating that he was speaking...

'Well fucking come in or git out. You're letting in all the bleeding flies mate.'

Ron quickly glanced around, noticing all the other flies buzzing around, and the fact the bat-wing doors were only from knee to head height.

His eyes widened with genuine fear as the old ringer removed his cigarette from his mouth, eyes bulging in a hostile gesture. He then coughed-up a mouthful of high-grade phlegm then spat at the spittoon parked at the base of the crude wooden pillar that was holding up the roof... and missed.

A deep gravel voice grunted from behind the bar, and Ron's head rapidly rotated to face the voice. Attention was now quickly directed to a big old man clutching a dirty cloth, busy polishing a wet beer glass.

His face was dark, and heavily wrinkled from many years of exposure to the harsh Australian sun. The long straggly grey hair on his head, flowed into his equally unkempt long beard. It was like looking at a picture of an old-time dirt miner of the eighteen hundreds... This was Harry, the owner of Sandfire Roadhouse.

All of a sudden he let out a bellowing shout...

'Hell, for Christ's sake Bluey. I told you before mate, if you can't improve yer fucking spit aim you're bloody-well out-o-here. You damn-well know we always like to keep this place bloody clean... that's yer last chance mate, then yer out.'

Then directing his attention to Ron and Pete, Harry changed his gruff manner in a fleeting instant, descending into a cheesy, wrinkled, and blackened tooth smile, crooning a tone of welcome...

'I'm Harry; I own this place, what will you two gentlemen like to drink. We have one kind of cold beer, Rum or Whisky; and I'll tell you blokes right now the water here is only fit fir washing, and putting out bloody bushfires.'

Ron's jaw was still in the fully dropped position, and therefore was not able to make an immediate and coherent reply, when from behind him Peter replied in a firm but clear voice...

'We'll have two large fucking cold beers thank you Harry.'

Peter had summed up the bar, the style, and language. Breaking the stiff and hostile atmosphere as the crowd now turned and resumed their normal drinking and talking.

Just then Ron noticed the sign at the end of the bar, next to the bundle of high-powered rifles stacked in the corner "order your food at the bar." He then asked Harry what was on the menu for dinner as he was starving and could eat a horse.

Harry squinted as he inspected his glass cleaning effort holding the glass up to the lonely dangling light bulb. Then grabbing another glass from the wooden shelf behind him. Then picking up the beer pistol he proceeded to fill both glasses while he expertly recited the menu.

'We got eggs, bacon, baked beans, and the last meat sausage.'

Harry rumbled as he thumped down on the wet bar two large frothing beers, slopping them all over the bar. Ron was quick to notice...

'That's breakfast Harry; it has gone five o'clock in the afternoon, what's for dinner old chap?' cocking his head to one side, offering an ear for the reply.

Harry drew a wheezy long sigh, leant forward on the beer soaked bar and smiled, revealing his two remaining blackened teeth. Ron felt the waft of his bad breath, and smelt his stale nicotine and beer-stained grey beard as Harry explained the delicate food issue at hand...

'The fat Greek is our day cook mate, and he's out back, tits-up blind fucking drunk. I only cook breakfast so do you blokes want something to eat or bloody not?'

Peter saved the day again, as Ron was still staring at Harry wide-eyed in speechless amazement...

'We'll have the lot each Harry, with tomato sauce if you have any,'

Harry snapped back quickly, eyeing them both with a surprising amount of cunning business shrewdness.

'What about that last sausage mate?'

Pete was just as quick.

'Just cut it in half Harry.' Harry's looked a bit confused.

'What, you only want half the bloody sausage?'

'No Harry, give the other half to my friend here who's choking on his beer.'

Ron was about to ruin everything by bursting out in loud laughter, when Harry had the last say...

'Coming up soon gentlemen, but the eggs could be a little off today being a couple of weeks old. I might have to swap the eggs for a chunk of horse steak... ya did say yer could eat a horse.'

Harry quickly turned, then disappeared through a dirty curtain into the back room.

This was exciting stuff, a real out-back stockman's pub, full of real characters that could have all been stars in Banjo Paterson's Clancy of the Overflow. Pete and Ron were warming to this pub, just as they were halfway through their second beer Harry arrived with the food.

In a surprising move, the locals all quickly removed there beer glasses from the long bar, and lent back as Harry skidded the metal breakfast plates, one after the other along the length of the beer wet bar. Harry had obviously done this many times before as the two plates arrived at their intended destinations spot-on, then he remarked.

'Get that lot into ya mates, yer won't get a feed like that in the City.'

Pete surveyed his tin plate noting the greasy bacon and large horse steak, with the largest sausage he had ever seen; all covered in baked beans, swimming in fat. He glanced across at Ron's plate hoping he could at least pass on half the huge sausage, but was disappointed to see Ron had a similar pile of food, and a similar sized sausage... This was the half sausage.

Harry was right; you won't get a feed like this in Perth, as the local health authorities would have closed him down instantly for serving such crap food to the public. Then again, both Peter and Ron were hungry, and after all it did smell good.

'You've forgotten the tomato sauce Harry.' Pete commented.

'No worries mate, coming right up.'

The food and the third large beer were going down well, when Ron, felt in a chatty mood. He had noticed the only vacant bar stool was next to an old man smoking a well-worn pipe; deciding in his own advancing age of thirty-nine that he could do with a sit down.

Being a car salesman, talking came easy to Ron.

'Hi, my names Ron, we're from Perth City; we've just driven up to see your beautiful Australian bush. What do you do around here... err... mate?'

The old man shifted around a bit on his bar stool to look at Ron. His eyes were squinted almost shut in his wrinkled, burnt face. Ron had assumed this was because of his ever present pipe smoke, as he had noticed the old man never removed the pipe from his mouth... not even to drink his beer with a rum chaser. His pipe was still in place as he replied in a threatening gruff voice.

'That's the Bull's stool yer on, nobody sits on Bull's bar-stool mate... not if you value yer fucking life that is.'

Ron was slowly absorbing this threat to his life at the same time removing his arse from the Bull's reserved stool. Looking up the bar noticing he had lost his previous place next to Pedro, Ron decided to stand

and chat to the old squinting man. Clasping his pipe for effect, the old man continued talking.

'The names Deadeye, I'm a roo shooter mate, I been shooting roos fir a living for mor'in forty years now. Another thing I just saved your life mate, around here a man git's a thank-you beer fir less than that.'

Ron was not slow, and quickly attracted Harry to buy the next round of beer, asking Harry why were there a number of powerful looking sporting rifles stacked behind the bar?

'Yer bloody-well drinking with the reason mate, bastards like Deadeye here and his Kangaroo-shooter mates get drunk and start shooting the fucking place up.'

Harry looked up and Ron followed his line of sight. It was only then Ron noticed the many bullet holes in the rusty corrugated iron roof. Trying to fit in with atmosphere and hide his rising terror, Ron shakily replied.

'It must be a fuck when it rains.'

Harry rumbled a modest reply in disgust.

'Tell me about it mate, I've replaced that tin roof three bloody times in the past nine years I've been here. It's a lucky thing we don't get much rain around here.'

Just then Peter ambled up looking for the gent's, three pints and he was now busting for a piss. The old man cocked his pipe in the direction of a sign hanging off the tin roof. It said in large letters "Piss Here" and someone had scrawled underneath "Best Grog in the West," and an arrow pointing in the general direction of the bar. A closer look revealed that the word "out" now covered with two crumpled business cards. The "Piss out Here" sign pointed to a door at the rear of the pub. Peter followed the arrow out the back door.

With Pedros urgent business needs resolved, Ron turned his attention back to the old roo shooter, who for the first time had removed the pipe from his mouth. He held an expression of utter surprise, or was it terror on his face.

His eyes were now wide open revealing a black hole where his left eye should have been. Ron had thought that "Deadeye" was referring to the old man's skills and ability with a rifle, being a Kangaroo shooter that is. Ron was wrong, and then the old man muttered the one word... 'Bull...'

Ron turned around to see one of the biggest men he had ever seen in his life. The Bull was having a quiet chat, looking down on a group of ringers. He was casually hanging on to a roof truss with one massive hand, sort of like hanging onto a city train commuter hold-strap, while swigging down a jug of beer with other. The four litre jug looked like a normal size beer handle glass in his huge fist.

A frightening two mad glaring eyes stared out of a face of thick black, frizzy hair. Only his bottom lip seen moving through the beer matted hair between swigs of his jug of beer.

Ron, again thanked the old roo shooter for the warning about the bar stool, and had to ask what line of business was the Bull in? The old man had replaced his pipe so he could talk normal again.

'He's a bull catcher mate, one of the best. They say he's as mad and cranky as a randy breeding bull that's missed out on a day's fucking. I've never seen him in a happy mood so I don't think he gets much pussy either these days.'

Ron stared at the Bull in amazement trying to visualise the act of normal copulation with this gorilla sized man... Peter had just returned from the loo with a look of puzzlement and fear on his face, distracting Ron from his strange fantasy thoughts. Peter burst out...

'I went out the back to find the men's toilet, and nearly fell into the bloody swimming pool. It's dark as a dog's guts out the back, there's only one little bulb dimly glowing over at the diesel power-generator hut.'

Ron looked genuinely worried, asking...

'What happened to you out there Peter?'

'Well I fumbled about in the dark and found a firm bit of concrete to stand on, then thought I might as well have a piss right here.

Everything was passing quite nicely as my eyes were gradually getting used to the dark, and then I looked down. I was standing right on the bloody edge of a big swimming pool, one more step and I would have been dead because it was empty, there was no water in it.'

Ron could see the stress in Peter's face. He had obviously had a very nasty shock. Then followed his eyes as he caught sight of the Bull. Peter's jaw dropping in amazement... whispering, 'would you look at the size of that bloke? Ron thought to calm Peter down a bit and distract him from any audible comment that might attract the Bull's attention.

'You need another beer Pete to steady your nerves. Any more of these close shaves with your life and you'll die of fright before we get you to Kununurra, that's two near misses you've had in four hours.'

Just then the old ringer's pipe started wobbling up and down, the old roo shooter was talking again. They both leant forward to hear what he had to say.

'I tell ya, Harry didn't want the pool mate, but the government wouldn't give him this bit o land for a Roadhouse unless he provided some sleeping dongas; sort of what you city slickers call a "Motel." He agreed to the dongas, but in the fine print he had to have that bloody big cement pond. Harry told them he barely had enough water out of the bore-hole for a wash let alone for a swimming pool.'

The old ringer paused to suck on his pipe which needed urgent attention. It made a strange crackling and hissing sound, then glowed a little with a short puff of smoke, when happy and all was going well he continued his story.

'Charlie borrowed a back-hoe from the Main Roads Department, and about ninety cubic yards of concrete, and Harry threw on a pile of free booze. Three weeks later we had this almighty great cement pond.'

Harry was listening in on this story and decided to tell the sad ending.

'We filled the fucker up with water, running my only water bore dry for a month in the process. Then

43

all the blokes and the staff had a bloody great party to celebrate the finished job.

Some of these bastards had never had a dunk in water in years. Few if any of these bastards could even swim. Everybody was so pissed; it's a wonder mate that we never lost a few of em.'

Ron and Peter were listening in awe to this great story, and then Pete asked what happened to all the water in the pool? In a quick clean-up, Harry ran his dirty towel over the wet bar, sniffed loudly up his nose and continued his story.

'A couple things didn't go to the bloody plan mate. For starters none of these shitheads had ever built a swimming pool before. The bloody pool wasn't even level, and the water just tipped out of one end. Then the worst fucking thing was these bastards had only worked on pouring concrete for storm-water culverts, yah know, for the main roads drainage.

Mate, it's no surprise the pool leaked like that bloody colander and strainer I have in the kitchen. I filled the bloody pool up once more the day before the government inspection bloke arrived so I could get the land title. We've never had water in it since, cept in the wet season. That was four years ago mate.'

An uncanny silence had fallen over the bar, all of whom were now listening in to Harry and his sad story. Harry had finished with a long pause, as no doubt everyone was quietly reminiscing about how the Sandfire Roadhouse was first born.

There was a scrape, and a loud squish and Ron turned around to see the Bull had taken-up residence, sitting on his reserved bar-stool. As Ron looked up at the Bull's massive head their eyes locked, Ron's in total terror as the Bull's mad staring eyes started to bore a hole into Ron's head.

The response and circumstances reminding him of the time he had teased a big male Gorilla for a bet at the Perth Zoo, except this-time the Gorilla was not behind any bars.

Ron nervously looked away, then down at his watch, and then croaked in a trembling voice.

'Shit Peter, we had better get back on the road, it has gone seven o'clock.'

Chapter: Four.

Just a bit of bad luck

Outside the Sandfire pub it was very dark, with only a hint of a moon. Ron pulled over to the three old style fuel pumps. The two floodlights, one each side of the row of fuel bowsers did little to offer much light, as they were thick with swarming insects, blocking most of the light. The petrol was pre-paid for with twenty dollars, but shut down as full at eighteen dollars. Harry had won again, with the tank full, they quickly got the Datsun 180 back onto the Great Northern Highway, heading for Broom.

Ron was driving slowly, about 125 kilometres an hour, every now and again washing the windscreen clear of the many bugs that decided to attack their car head on. Peter had been thinking, and decided to share what was on his mind with Ron.

'You know; Bill's a lot faster than us, he probably thought that we are still ahead of him. My guess is he's going at it like a mad-man trying to catch us up, he'll most likely be in Kununurra by now.'

Staring into the darkness Ron nodded his head in agreement, then added,

'If that's the case; you might be safe for a while, at least Bill won't be running you over before we reach Kununurra.'

The Broome turn-off Roadhouse came into view. This was a much more modern fuelling station. Many rows of semi-trailers and cattle road trains, covered the massive parking hard stand in neat lines. Peter appeared fascinated by how close each truck parked to one another, with barely enough room to walk between them.

Most trucks were five trailers long, hence the name "road train," with the mooing and the stench of hot distressed cattle, all going into the Derby meatworks to be processed. Peter reckoned they all knew they were about to be slaughtered. Ron was not listening to Peter's ramblings and had other more important matters on his mind, and his nose, as such he decided to park upwind on the other side of the parking area to avoid most of the stink.

The Broome Highway Roadhouse, being well lit and fitted with modern fuel pumps. It also had a glass fronted eating place full of truck drivers, with a juke box blasting out the Beatles music.

This was a noticeable difference to Harry's bush style Roadhouse; however, the masses of swarming insects around all the light poles were the same. The only difference was this brightly lit Roadhouse attracted far more flying pests. Maybe old Harry wasn't so dumb after all.

With the Datsun refuelled Pete led the way to the café and was startled at the action of the automatic glass sliding door and the blast of air-conditioning,

'No bat-wing doors on this place' mused Pete as he breezed through the door,

'And no spittoons either remarked Ron.'

However all the people inside café and bar including those serving behind the bar counter looked and acted very much the same, the voice from behind the bar counter was far louder than the music.

'What'll you two bastards have ta drink then mates eh, what's your poison. We have one cold beer on tap and two canned beers Emu bitter and Carlton draft or Whisky or Bundy Rum; so what'll it be then mate?'

Pete thought to himself, indeed very up-market then replied softly.

'Just two bottles of Coca-Cola please.'

The welcome voice complete with a cigarette stained smile was gone in an instant. This was a man's country, and men drank beer, lots of it, and as for coke that used only as an additive to whisky or rum. The look on the fat bartender's dirty month-old, unshaved face said it all. These two were a couple of city poofters or worse... most likely Government abattoir health inspectors.

The barman slammed the two bottles of Coca-Cola down hard on to the heavy wooden topped bar leaving Pete and Ron to open them with the hope they would all be covered in the stuff. Ron eyed this large dim-witted oaf with a warm sly smile and said.

'We've changed our mind old chap, we'll have two cans of Emu beer instead thank you. We're also looking for our friend who is travelling alone ahead of us in a pea-green Leyland motorcar. He's a thickset bloke, about 25 years old with two bandages on his head, a miserable look on his face and speaks with a pommy accent.'

The bartender lightened up a bit and resumed the greasy smile again.

'Yeh I think I remembers a bloke like that about three hours ago. Don't know anything about a pea-green car though, and I've never heard of a Leyland, only Land-Rover, Toyota's, and Holden's around here mate. This bloke who was ear drank half a bottle of Bundy rum at the bar, and took a full bottle with him.'

Both Pete and Ron said aloud together, as in one voice.

'That's our mate Bill Gump.'

Pete turned to head for the door, and accidentally bumped into a large truckie in standard truckie dress, dirty blue singlet, black footy shorts, and steel capped work-boots, arms all covered in poor quality tattoos. He was making a dash for the bar...

'Just watch where you're fucking-well going shit-head.'

Pushing Peter roughly to one side in his rush for the bar, yelling at the barman above the loud music.

'Hey you, dung-head, four double rum and cokes, and make it bloody snappy.'

Just as Ron and Pete were going through the glass exit door, there was a loud hissing sound, then? "Shit on a fucking bastard" as the truckie became showered in Coca-Cola, followed by much laughing from the crowd at the bar.

Back at the Datsun 180B a Toyota Landcruiser pulled up alongside with "Stock Inspector" on the door. The stout looking Aboriginal man politely tipped back his akubra hat...

'Which way you boys going?' he asked in a quiet Australian drawl.

'We're heading for Fitzroy Crossing, hoping to get there before eleven o'clock to meet up with our friend; we're staying at the lodge.'

'Be careful mate, I just come from Fitzroy there are a lot of stray cattle on the road at this time of the year. I just gone pulled two dead beasts off the road not more than an hour ago. You wouldn't stand much of a chance in a toy car like yours, not without a real bull-bar on the front mate.'

Pete asked the question Ron was thinking.

'Didn't by any chance pass a pea-green Leyland P76 heading for Fitzroy?'

The stock inspector thought for a moment stroking his chin while looking for an inspirational reply, and then asked.

'A Leyland's a pommy truck ain't it? Didn't see no truck but then again mate it's a bloody dark night, but I did have some stupid bastard at the Fitzroy end try to run me off the road. The bloke only had one headlight working, and that was on bloody high beam.'

Peter and Ron thanked the stock inspector and headed out on to the gravel road again.

One thing about driving at night on bush roads is you can see the glow of any oncoming vehicles headlights a very long way off, both from the front and the rear, but then again. Big black Brahman bulls don't have any headlights, and as Bill was soon to find out, no tail-lights either.

The stock inspector was right, as there were quite a few cattle and kangaroos on the highway trying to say hello to them on the way to Fitzroy Crossing. Ron said he wondered how Bill was going as he was feeling the strain keeping a good look-out for cattle, and between them they had four eyes to assist in this task.

Pete was more concerned that the one eyed vehicle that almost ran the stock inspector off the road might have been Bill. That idea rapidly faded as the lights of Fitzroy Crossing came into view, they were both looking forward to a good night's sleep.

At this late hour of eleven, they were both relieved to see the Fitzroy Lodge reception was still open and bright. The Aboriginal nightshift bloke at the reception desk was quietly thumbing through a well-used porn magazine with a beer in hand. Then with a wide toothless grin...

'Hi der boss, what can ah do fir you cobbers tonight?'

He was happy enough although Ron did suspect that he had interrupted him at an important part of his porn delight. Leaning on the counter a tired Ron sighed.

'Look we're sorry we're a bit late; but we do have a room booked in the name of Richins.'

The receptionist ran his finger expertly up and down the booking register, then confidently turning pages, and announcing with a puckered lip sigh...

'Sorry mate, you don't have no booking here, but that's ok mate, we got a room for fifty bucks cash. Just the one night is it, an only one room? You blokes gonna sleep together eh?'

As the native receptionist turned around to unhook a key from the board Ron leant over the counter and turned the register page back...

'Here we are old chap, last entry right there, "Mr Richins room for two; the smart ass requests a room with a sea view," that's us. The look on the receptionists face was that of a small boy having just been caught with his hand in the cookie jar. The moment was full of doubt and suspicion, when suddenly a voice from behind them broke the uncomfortable silence.

'Thanks for standing in for me mate, I'll take over from here Brumby, grab yourself another beer on your way out.'

Then turning to greet them, the well-dressed man in his pink shirt, jeans and quality leather sandals smiled...

'Did I hear you say a Mr Richins? There's been a bloke asking about you guys, he's been in here three or four times now, looks like he's been in an accident or two.'

Ron required a little further identification.

'Is this bloke short and solid built, and got two bandages stuck on his forehead with a miserable look on his face and a pommy accent?' The receptionist pouted his lips and looked a little puzzled.

'Yea sounds like the same guy cep't this bloke's also got his arm in a sling and sporting a brand new metal nose splint and has two really bad black eyes.'

Ron and Peter were still looking at the receptionist's matter-of-fact face when a loud bellowing voice blasted at them from behind them.

'Where the fuck have you two bastards been?'

The receptionist tilted his chin in the direction of the voice, confirming.

'That's the bloke I was talking about.'

No need to turn around they both knew this was indeed Bill who was fuming, when they did turn to meet face-to-face they were both stunned. Bill was standing in the well-lit entry foyer; his shirt covered in blood with more down his legs.

His left arm was in a sling with a tightly bound bandage around his wrist and he was still sporting the two medi-tape bandages, one each side of his forehead. That was the good bit. Bill also had two massive black eyes, and a shiny metal splint that was obviously supporting a painfully broken nose.

Both Ron and Pete chorused together "what the fuck happened to you?" Bill took a swig from his bottle of rum and gave out a long sad sigh...

'Just a bit of bad luck I suppose. I was hammering along the gravel road about one hundred and eighty kilometres an hour. Trying to catch up with you lot when I ran slap-bang into two of the biggest fucking cattle you ever seen; a bull and a bloody cow...'

Pete just had to interrupt Bill's story, as for some reason he needed to know more detail about this point.

'How did you know it was a bull and a cow, I mean it could have been two cows, or two bulls, after all it was dark?'

Everybody looked at one another in amazement, Ron declaring indignantly.

'What the bloody hell does it matter what make of cattle it was Pete. I mean it's not important is it?'

The receptionist spoke; he was now wearing his slim, (I'm very intelligent style glasses) propped on the very end of his thin nose Looking over the top he said.

'Well I sure as hell would like to know mate?'

They all turned to Bill who was by this time highly frustrated, and about ready to explode at his friends for trivialising his near escape from death... Then blurted out what he considered was obvious.

'Well that was easy to know, because the two of them were fucking like mad cows do in the middle of the bloody road, in utter exotic bliss. I hit the bull in the arse so hard; he went up over the top of the P76. Bouncing off the roof, and then the cow slid up the bonnet arse-first right through the front windscreen, filling my new car with cow shit.'

Everybody was now giving Bill their full attention, trying to picture this very tragic, and yet very funny situation. Pete was still after much more detail of this strange event.

'What happened to your nose and wrist?'

Bill had calmed down a bit now and was now looking his usual glum self.

'Here's a bit more of my bad luck mates. When I bought the P76, I had decided on the lap belt only choice, instead of the full lap and sash seatbelt alternative. I was trying to save a couple of hundred bucks on the price of my new car.

The lap only belt was great for stopping my head hitting the roof, and when I hit the potholes in the road. Only thing was when I hit the bulls arse, my car went from 180 kilometres an hour to zero in about five metres.

The lap belt held me in place but the rest of my body catapulted forward, smashing my face hard on to the steering wheel and dashboard breaking my nose in the bloody process.

I strained my wrist when I held my arm up to protect my head; my head and nose then hit my wrist.'

Bill looked at his well bandaged wrist with a truly miserable look, and then continued in a sad sorrowful voice.

'I've been sitting in the local hospital waiting room for hours. They thought I had been in a drunken fight and were waiting until I sobered up before fixing this lot,' holding up his many wounds...

Bill was not a happy man... at all. Just then came a long low whistle from the amazed receptionist...

'You're one hell-of-a tough bloke mate.'

Then Ron added.

'You mean one hell-of-a tough head, anyway how's you're P76, it must be a write-off then?'

Bill looked so sad; we all thought he was going to cry. This had been a harrowing day for us all, except for the receptionist who then joyfully enquired.

'Well-then, just how is your car mate; adding with a look of glee on his face. Is she totally buggered?

'I drove the bastard here didn't I,' snapped Bill. 'That fuck-up was over seventy kilometres down the road, all the front of my car is caved in with a busted headlight, but she still goes okay.'

Pete and Ron looked at each other, thinking about the Aboriginal Stock Inspectors near miss by some idiot with only one headlight... Bill continued with his sad story.

'The bonnet and roof's stuffed, and the windscreen is smashed, also the complete exhaust system was ripped off. The whole car now smells of cow shit. Other than that it drives ok, it'll get me to Kununurra.' Then Bill sadly added.

'My head hurts; I feel I could sleep for a week.'

Peter was staring at Bill with a sympathetic look on his face, and then mumbled.

'That P76 is only just two weeks old. If it ever gets to Kununurra I suppose it will be the only Leyland P76 in the whole of the North-West of Australia, who the hell's going to fix all the body damage up here in the remote North-West?'

A new day brings new challenges. Everybody was up by seven thirty but missed the breakfast; there was nothing left. Bill stood in the dining room glaring at all the empty trays in the bain-marie, the smell was there but the food was gone, this just made Bill all the madder.

He was about to go and complain to the little fat bloke at the door who had made the smart-arsed comment, "first in best-dressed matey." Ron quietly reminded him that he had bunked down in their room for free, and was not entitled to any breakfast; anyway Ron had a better idea. He had noticed the blackfella who was on the reception last night was now in the kitchen washing-up.

'Hi there Brumby remember me? Looks like we're a bit late for breakfast, any chance of rustling something up for three hungry blokes that can keep their mouths shut about sly cash for rooms and such things?'

Brumby was no dill as he quickly got the measure of the situation. He most certainly didn't want his boss to know about his slight-of-hand fifty dollar cash along the finger room deals. Brumby gave Ron the thumbs up sign and then put his finger to his lips for him to be quiet. He then turned to the cook who was lighting another cigarette from his old butt.

'Marv mate, I bin just find out dat dem der fellas in da breakfast rooms is Federal meat inspectors from Derby and on da way home to da Can-berra mate. We shuda give em a good breakfast keep em in a good mood, I kin start cooking now.'

Marv took a deep drag on his new fag, and looked out of the kitchen slide, then caught sight of Bill. His eyes opened wide with smoke cascading out of all the holes in his head then he said...

'Looks like one of them fell into the cattle holding yards, and got mauled by an angry bull, he looks pretty messed up, and he don't look very happy either mate.

I think you're right Brumby, let's get em a good breakfast before they decide to shut down the Derby meatworks... then we'd all be out of a bloody job'

Bill announced that the breakfast was the best he could remember in a long-time, well not since the truckie-stop breakfast, and even managed a painful smile, which looked rather odd on his badly bruised face.

Peter enquired if Bill could manage to drive all right since he only had one arm left and both his eyes were all but shut from the massive blow to his head. Bill assured Pete and Ron that without a windscreen he would have to drive with his eyes almost shut against the wind, gravel, and dust. As for his damaged left arm, well he only ever drove with one hand on the wheel anyway.

Ron could see that Pete had a grim look on his face, and quickly guessed that he had not forgotten his close brush with death. Bill still not forgiven for the Sandfire Roadhouse attempt on his life. Too late, Peter blurted out a meaningful suggestion to Bill. That being, he might try keeping both of his hands-on the steering wheel and both eyes on the fucking road to avoid running people, and animals over... Then Ron saved the day by stepping in with a well-timed diversion.

'Right then lads; let's get this bloody show back on the road. We've got 410 miles to drive if we're going to get to Kununurra today.'

Bill stopped walking towards his badly bent P76, stared at the ground and said in a thoughtful voice.

'I make that distance at 660 kilometres, that's only a slow five hours driving. We should easily be in Kununurra by two o'clock,'

Ron's eyebrows shot up, then added to his imperial calculations.

'That's if you don't hit another bleeding randy bull on the way, and hang-on their Bill, that's averaging around seventy-five miles an hour. I think we'll both see you much later in this day at Kununurra Mister Bill Gump.'

Well folks, that's just what happened. Peter and Ron met up with Bill in the Kununurra Hotel at around half past three. Bill was sitting alone at one end of the long bar caressing a large beer. All the locals were up the other end of the bar looking at Bill's and his injuries in awe. They were no doubt trying to guess whether he had been hit by a train, driven through a wall, or hit a large bull with his car. Little did they know it was in fact all three?

Chapter: Five.

That was bad luck too

I could hear the raised voices in the outer office and guessed that Peter my brother-in-law had finally arrived from Perth. It was just after four thirty. Lesley, my lovely wife and I were just about to go home early after a 5am early start sorting out our messy business books.

Well this was good news for us. Peter could now take on some of our busy mechanical workshop load as our new service manager. Being my brother-in-law I could hear that Lesley was all excited in the outer office. I opened the door to a sea of smiling faces.

'Hi there Pedro (my pet name for Peter as we had two other Peter's working for us) the bar is in here, there's only the office girl out there,' nodding my head toward Lesley.

Pedro's sister screwed her face up at me, then noticing the casual Ron propped against the door frame like Frank Sinatra.

'I see you brought that mad pommy rally driver with you.'

The conversation was drying up fast, then noticing their tired and weary looks, while smiling and handshaking vigorously all around.

'You both look well and truly stuffed, how was the trip up from Perth?'

Pedro and Ron looked at each other with a (you can-tell-him) look, and then Ron suggested a small diversion from the answer, providing a better solution.

'Did I hear you say there's a bar in your office?'

'Gentlemen will you all please walk this way,' I gestured, leading them into my office faking a pronounced limp, all of us now limping in a line the same way like the silly idiots in a skit from a Spike Milligan show.

Drinks in hand, Pedro and Ron were now in their natural habitat, and state of relaxation. They went on to explain that their friend Bill Gump had decided to follow them up to the Kimberley's in his new Leyland P76 Targa Florio, just for a couple of weeks holiday. I had heard of this Bill Gump before, Pedro had mentioned Bill in conversation's a few times on the phone, mainly about some bad-luck car accidents down in Perth.

Pedro went on to say matter-of-factly that Bill had just recently lost his job at Johnson Motors for backing a local Doctors brand new Triumph PI car through the service workshop solid brick wall. Then he casually said that he may be staying in Kununurra a little longer than previously planned.

I was thinking poor bugger, then the thought occurred to me I've never seen the new Leyland P76, well only in a photo, and this was also the top of the line model. The Targa Florio no less... turning to Pedro I enquired.

'Well where's Bill now, still on the way up to Kununurra?' Pedro gave Ron that you-tell-him look again.

'Well no, not exactly Niven, he's actually just outside, down in the workshop checking out all your new garage equipment; you know, as mechanics do.'

'For god's sake guys,' I said, 'call him up and give the bloke a drink, what's wrong with you guys?'

Pedro walked across to the window overlooking the workshop and banged on the glass, then pointed to his drink, and waved his hand for Bill to come up to the office. Ron said Bill drinks Bundy rum and coke, a lot of it, so I went about pouring a very large strong mix. Ron and Pedro were oddly quiet as I heard Lesley give out a muffle a gasp.

I looked up from my bar work to see a look of terror on her face, through the open door in the adjoining office, a second later Bill appeared in the doorway. I had never met Bill before. I was speechless for that moment then gathering myself together at the sight, remembering this bloke had just recently driven a car through a brick wall...

'Shit Bill; if you don't mind me saying so you look like you've been run over by a train, try this it'll make you feel a lot better,' offering Bill the potent rum drink.

Bill was confused, should he take the drink and have no spare hand to shake my hand, or shake first and then grab the drink. I could see what his immediate problem was. I had figured out the social mechanical problem in a flash, then putting Bill's drink on the bar, I grabbed Bills outstretched hand. His grip was like a vice and I pretended not to winch at the pressure. Bill's face cracked into a frightening twisted smile, and then he spoke.

'Good to meet you Niven, Peter's told me a lot about you.'

With welcome relief he released my hand, he then reached out and retrieved the large rum and coke off the bar; after a long sip he continued.

'About that train crash, it wasn't entirely fault you know... I wasn't even the driver, I was just left to... well just die.'

Bill took a breath to continue his defensive story... Ron and Pedro both broke into his conversation at the same time, cutting Bill's confession off in midsentence.

'Bill, tell Niven all about your new P76 and how well it went on the way up the Great Northern Highway.' Ron managed to get out first...

'Yes tell him all about your new P76,' Pedro echoed like a well-trained parrot.

Bill's almost closed black eyes opened a little more and sparkled to match the attempted grin, and then launched into the story of his beloved car.

'Best car I've ever owned, she can sit on 170 clicks an hour all daylong and she's as steady as a bloody rock. On top of that she covered the 630 kilometres from Hedland to Broome on one tank full of fuel, that's around ten litres of petrol each hundred kilometres, for a 4.4 litre V8 engine that must be close to a record. I don't even think Ron's shitty little four cylinder Datsun could beat that for economy.'

I was totally impressed, this sounded like the perfect vehicle for Australia. I was getting quite excited about seeing this car in the flesh. My excitement must have been obvious as Pedro perked up...

'Bill has to go to the hospital now to get all his many wounds checked out. If you could give him directions on how to get there; you never know with a bit of luck, they might keep him in for a couple days. Ron and I could do with a few stress-free days... and an early night.'

Bill gave Pedro a stony look but remained silent. I offered Bill a bed for the night but he declined saying that he had taken up an offer from a bloke he had met in the pub. Pedro and Ron followed Lesley and I back to the house, and after a few hours of chatting and drinking, they both bunked down in my spare room for the night.

Work starts at six am… at that time it's still dark in the tropics. I was long gone before Pedro, and Ron passed their first wind for the day. At around seven Bill walked into the office, he looked far worse than I remembered from yesterday, not a smile in sight, then in an effort to cheer things up.

'Hi there, good morning Bill, you look like you slept in your car last-night?'

Bill slumped into a chair looking exhausted. I yelled out to Fay the hire car hostess and office girl to make Bill a cup of strong coffee, and quickly before he dies on us. This would not be good for our business image at all. Bill managed a weak smile and a dismal comment.

'Christ I don't look that bad do I, any chance of using your shower before the coffee arrives?'

'That's fine Bill, the ablutions are directly below where I am sitting; meanwhile I'll go outside and have a look at your magnificent P76 Targa Florio.'

Bill obviously did not hear my last comment, and struggled out of his chair making his way to the door; he then stopped, and turned. With a long sad face he softly murmured in my direction...,

'By the way you were right Niv; I did sleep in my car last night.'

As Bill left the office I thought why didn't he just take-up my offer of a bed.

This was a very complicated bloke indeed... I was soon to find out much more complicated than I could have ever imagined.

As I went past the lunch room, Fay handed me a nice cup of strong black coffee. I then made my way through the mechanical workshop where the mechanics had already started on the day's workload.

Two bare hairy legs fitted with steel cap safety boots seen poking out from under a jacked-up Landcruiser on stands. A loud cursing bellow, followed by a metallic clanking came from the mechanic working under the Toyota.

'Morning Greg, I hear you're in a happy mood this morning. I have good news, my brother-in-law Pedro has finally arrived. We don't want to scare him away this early in his new job, so I thought we should give him a few days to settle in, and then we'll put him to work. Oh by the way, you didn't by chance see one of those new fancy Leyland P76' cars around?'

There was another loud clang as Greg's spanner slipped and fell onto the concrete floor again, and then more cursing and silence... then he answered.

'There's a green Leyland parked just outside the front door boss, I thought it was just another bloody repair job.'

The clanking resumed telling me that Greg had said all he had to say for now, which was more than he would normally have to say... on anything. I tried to continue our conversation, adding...

'No Greg that's Pedro's friend's car, his name is Bill Gump. He came up for a few weeks holiday, he's a very nice bloke I'll introduce you to him later.'

I continued my way through the big front sliding doors then the P76 came into view. My full cup of coffee slipped from my fingers at the sight.

The car was well and truly smashed-up. The complete front of the car being all pushed in; the bonnet crumpled and tied down with a piece of fencing wire.

The windscreen was missing and the roof caved in with a complete exhaust system tied on to the crumpled roof, again with number six fencing wire. Looking inside revealed a mass of broken windscreen glass, much blood everywhere and large dollops of cow shit, which stank because of being quite fresh.

My brain was slowly taking in all the damage to this new Leyland P76, just as Pedro and Ron pulled up alongside in their Datsun 180B Sport XXX, having just been washed, and did not have a scratch.

'What the fuck happened to Bill's new pride and joy P76?'

Pedro looked a bit worried at my sudden blast of enquiry. Ron leapt in, the ever-ready car salesman, answered with his accomplished beaming smile and convincing reply.

'Oh we were going to tell you about Bills little car accident last night, but we were all too tired, it was a very long day yesterday. I guess the short story is Bill hit a bull and a cow just before Fitzroy Crossing. As you can see it made a right old mess of his new P76.'

I thought about that for a second.

'Crikey, was Bill in two separate cattle road accidents then, a bull and then a cow?'

'Nope, only the one, one big accident, it was in the dark when Bill ran into the arse of a bull that just happened to be fucking a cow. You might say a sort of small profile, hard to see just a bull's arse in the dark. Easy to understand when you visualize all the details… it was a very long day yesterday.'

Ron's matter of fact detail and patter was the same as if he were trying to sell me a new car. This brought further urgent questions to my mind. I didn't think bulls fornicated at night in the dark. I always thought they were daytime fuckers? This must be a very rare accident indeed? To come across a bull that was so randy, that it found the need to satisfy its lust for a cow in the middle of the night, in the middle-of-the-road.

Very unlucky indeed, then again, I remembered that Bill had just recently driven a new Triumph motor car straight through a solid brick wall at his last workplace. Well that was unlikely and unlucky too.

'You mean to say Ron; that it was a long and dangerous day for poor Bill.' Then thinking aloud...

'Just how much of Bill's many injuries were caused by hitting the bull, as against driving the car through the workshop brick wall?'

Pedro and Ron looked sheepishly away. I could tell they were trying to avoid replying to my question; both saved by the timely arrival of Bill...

'Good morning guys, I hope you both slept well last night, because I certainly didn't in the back of my P76 full of broken glass and cow shit.'

I could tell straight away that Bill was not at all happy. He had; as I was later to understand, resumed his standard grim manic view on the world. Bill then turned to me with my answer...

'My crushed wrist, broken nose, and the two black eyes were caused when I hit the bloody bull. The large bump on the right side of my head was done when I drove through a brick wall at work, and the other large bump on my head was when...'

Just then Pedro quickly interjected Bill's flowing story.

'Have you had any breakfast yet Bill, it's nearly eight o'clock you must be starving, let's go up town and grab something to eat.'

Ron was just about to say that they both had breakfast at my house, when I noticed a distinct glint in Bill's almost closed black eyes, and the start of a faint, but painful smile. Bill had been expertly side-tracked by the simple thought of food, then turning to Pedro in a sudden change of attitude.

'That sounds like a bloody good idea to me, let's go right now.'

Pedro knew Bill's weak spot... food; the boys climbed back into the Datsun and headed into town. I picked up my broken coffee cup and headed back into the workshop. It was nice of them to think of Bill, as Pedro and Ron would have most certainly had breakfast at my house. Then I wondered what Bill was about to say, it would have been interesting as to what had caused that other big bump on his forehead?

Bill eventually managed to find cheap single men's accommodation in the town. The Leyland P76 then taken to the local panel shop for an insurance claim and repairs. Kununurra being a recently built and a modern designed town, it was easy to walk to all of the most important places such as the pub, tavern, the social club, and the hospital.

The weeks flashed by and Ron eventually returned to Perth, and Pedro had settled into his new job managing the mechanical workshop. I had no idea that Bill was coming up to Kununurra with Pedro. Unfortunately I had employed another mechanic only a few weeks prior to their arrival, as such there was not enough work available to offer Bill a job. Pedro would have told Bill about this situation.

Eventually I found Bill a mechanics job with Foraco Drilling, a French exploration company drilling for anything valuable. This company had been looking for a local mechanic for some time, someone who would be happy to help their mechanics. To work in the bush carrying out mechanical work on their drilling rig equipment, working in both the bush, and their town depot.

One of the main problems confronted by previous locally hired people was that, other than the operations manager Denis Bosquet; none of the Foraco drilling crew could speak a word of English. Somehow, why we will never know, Bill proved to be the perfect man for the job.

Chapter: Six.
The flying Mini Moke

Foraco Drilling was an all French national crewed drilling company, managed by Denis Bosquet, a thirty-one year-old French geologist. Denis spoke perfect English with a delightful French accent, and was married to an equally delightful lady called Ida, having two beautiful young daughters, completing the perfect young family. They were fortunate enough to rent a Government Agricultural department house, only a few houses down the street from our house. Therefore, we socialised with the Bosquet family on a regular basis, the girls, Lesley and Ida all got along well.

Denis worked long hours, and was under immense pressure from his company to complete his drilling programme on time, and within budget. The smaller Foraco Drilling Company was part of the huge French government owned Elf Aquitaine Drilling Exploration conglomerate.

Both had large and extensive drilling programmes in the Kimberley region. From what I was told and understood, Foraco being the smaller and the more mobile drilling rig, their main job being to test drill for likely sites, and provide the sample information for the big Aquitaine reverse cycle drilling rig. They would then go back after a drill-hole was completed and carry out Gamma-ray logging of the hole.

Aquitaine were looking for oil, and had produced some encouraging test results on the Ningbing tidal flats, this area being directly north of Kununurra, and the irrigated cotton farm area. Most of the drill holes had struck massive deposits of gas, and this was the conversation most talked about down at the pub.

Aquitaine would be required under their Australian exploration licence to cap off these high pressure gas-holes with what's called a "Christmas tree," the name for a pressure valve stack. This procedure cost them a considerable amount of their exploration budget and time, all in an effort to make the gas holes safe. At this time a German geologist, Doctor Reinhardt Ramdor, managed the Elf Aquitaine Australian drilling program.

In my experience with the French, they don't have much time for the British and like the Germans even less. It came as quite a surprise to us all when the new Elf Aquitaine operations manager turned out to be a German, especially since like Foraco just about all the Aquitaine drilling crew were French nationals.

The new Aquitaine German operations manager change-over had taken place a few months back, before

Pedro and Bill had arrived in Kununurra, this would be Aquitaine's third operations manager in less than two years. Rinehart was a very different character to previous operations manager Peter, who was a sort of laid-back kind of a guy and cared more for his two large Alsatian dogs than drilling holes in the ground.

I will never forget my first involvement with Peter, shortly after Peter had arrived in Kununurra taking up the position as operations manager for Aquitaine. My dog Shan (Welsh name for John) went over to Peter's house to try his luck with Peter's Alsatian bitch. Peter took a very dim view of my blue-heeler ridgeback cross trying to mount his pure bread Alsatian, and offered Shan an irresistible chunk of steak... filled with rat poison.

Peter was later seen that day dumping Shan's body out at the local rubbish tip, the sad event eventually reported back to me. Everybody in town knew my dog Shan, as he was quite a character in his own right. Well it goes without saying that Peter and I never did get along after that, as such I did little business with Aquitaine during Peter's time as the boss.

When Doctor Reinhardt Ramdor replaced Peter, I thought that this was going to be a good start to a new friendship, and with luck the renewing of my lost business with Aquitaine. Reinhardt and his family had arrived in the January of what proved to be a record heavy and very wet monsoon season.

He got off to a very impressive start, using new in-field deep-drilling techniques, unknown to this area.

However, he would quickly learn that pushing the Aquitaine drilling programme hard in the middle of a Kimberley tropical wet season is not very productive or good idea, and is always a very expensive exercise. Rinehart was the smart man, sent from France to resolve and fix both the major Aquitaine drilling problems of gaining higher production results, and reducing company expenses.

I liked Reinhardt. He was the typical well educated German who spoke perfect English, and as I understand perfect French, all with a crisp uppercut High German accent. He was about 37 years old and obviously from a good class academic family background. Now under pressure and expected to perform, and produce impressive results in keeping with his well respected and documented family.

This urgency to shine in the field of geology was most important to Doctor Reinhardt, and the cause of some almighty Elf Aquitaine geological drilling blunders. One such blunder included my company... and at great cost to me.

Shortly after assuming the powerful position as Kimberley operations manager for Elf Aquitaine Australia, Reinhardt changed the drilling programme to a different, and what he considered was a more promising location. All the crew thought they would be standing down their drilling operations for a few weeks because of the heavy monsoon, but Reinhardt had decided on another strategy. That strategy was to simply press on with the current drilling programme.

Two weeks into Reinhardt's new drilling programme, the Kimberley experienced one of the largest continued monsoonal downpours I can ever remember. The rain bucketed down for days on end, flooding the Kimberley and top end, washing out all the roads, and cutting off the town of Kununurra. Only the local airport offered some form of limited access, but only until the airport bulk aviation fuel ran out... or was water contaminated.

The Aquitaine drilling rig was now totally cut-off and isolated, now only accessible by helicopter. Both of my Toyota Landcruiser 4X4 vehicles hired to Aquitaine were firmly bogged down in the bush somewhere, and totally unreachable.

The drill rig crew had little choice, expected to stay with the rig and carry-on as best they could. Expensive helicopter charter was now the only way of flying in all food and provisions, and then the unimaginable happened. The massive 6,000 gallon drill-rig water-truck had suddenly become totally and unmovably bogged.

Now a drill-rig this size requires water to mud-lubricate, cool, flush-out the drill tip, and the drilling rods. Without huge amounts of water the thing just can't work, diamond drill-tips will burn-out and twelve-inch diameter steel drill rods will twist off in the hole like wet drinking straws.

The fifteen man drill crew work two shifts none stop twenty-four hours a day and are being paid big money. Doctor Reinhardt Ramdor now had a very big problem to solve with his smart Germanic mind. This Aquitaine drilling rig was one of the largest transportable drilling rigs in the world. The drill equipment was designed and built to Aquitaine's special requirements, then a leading world-class technology in reverse cycle, hammer headlong drilling.

With all the water that came out of the sky that caused this massive problem, one would think that a water shortage could never have been a foreseeable problem. However, it was, and then Reinhardt had this brilliant all German idea.

Reinhardt had noticed that a number of the cotton farmers were using a modified 44 gallon fuel drum in the back of a standard mini-moke for spraying crops. He had decided this was a great way to get water to the drill-rig, and so he called me to arrange for the hire of a mini-moke. I was at the pub having lunch when the phone call came through to the bar...

'Goot afternoon Niven, you 'aff no doubt heard of mine vater bogging problem, I now 'aff ze solution, and you mine friend can be of help. Mine excellent plan is zer simple. I will send by jet helicopter one of your most reliable mini-Mokes an't a 210 litre drum out to ze drill-rig to ferry vater. Zis may be a small amount of vater but enough to keep ze rig going until they can free ze large vater truck. Ze distance to water is only one kilometre. Three trips per hour iz 630 litres an hour, enough water I think to keep ze drill-rig running.'

I thought about this for all of a second, it didn't sound like a good idea to me at all, and so decided to poke holes in Reinhardt's silly water carting idea.

'Reinhardt, a mini-moke weighs about 490 kilos and the best lifting chopper we have in this area is Vowell Air-services MD500C. That's the one that has been airlifting materials and wet concrete to the top of Kelly's Knob for the construction of the new ABC radio broadcast tower. This chopper can only lift about 600 kilos in total at a standard ambient temperature of 25c. By the time you add the weight of the pilot and two hours fuel with a local temperature of around 40c, I doubt it could lift a moke. Then you would have the other problem that a mini-moke will get bogged just a fast as any other vehicle in this tropical mud bath.'

There was a short pause and a long sigh. It was obvious that Reinhardt suffered fools badly. He had already worked out the answers to all my possible criticisms of his water carting German master plan.

'One moment please, I am not ze fool Niven, I am aware of ze lift capacity of ze MD 500 helicopter. My intention is with your permission to disassemble ze mini-moke unt transport out ze parts, one by one to ze drill-rig, I must have your answer now as ze helicopter is standing by.'

I could tell that Reinhardt was determined his plan would work. Nothing I said would dissuade him this was a bad idea, and then thinking the hire business was very slow at this time of the year... why not... but I had some firm conditions in mind.

'I will agree to this plan Reiny, on condition that you pay for my mechanics to dismantle and reassemble the mini-moke. In addition, that you also pay a flat rate per day as the vehicle will not be clocking up many kilometres. You must also agree to take full responsibility for the vehicle being used in a remote area and for any possible damage.'

'Das ist agreed, now ve must hurry.'

I strolled back to the workshop and had Greg the mechanic pull one of the hire Mokes apart. Then place all the bits on our vehicle break-down recovery trailer. I then instructed him to take the trailer load of Moke bits down to the airport...

I could tell Greg thought I had gone mad, but as usual he said nothing, then went about pulling one of my newest Mokes apart. Reinhardt agreed that Bill Gump would fly out and assemble the Moke out at the Aquitaine drill camp.

All was going well. Reinhardt reluctantly signed the hire contract. As such, the first sling-load went out to the stranded rig, hanging off the choppers steel sling being a load of five wheels, battery, the windscreen, and the bonnet.

The next part was the main body, engine, and suspension. This was too much weight for the Hughie; the helicopter could lift the load off the ground, but could not travel without losing height and the Moke hitting the ground.

Reinhardt insisted on several attempts however all failed. I suggested that we simply remove the engine and sub-assembly and send them out as two separate parts. Much to Reinhardt's reluctance, he in the end accepted this non German solution. The second sling-load went out to the rig only twenty minutes chopper flying time from the Kununurra airport.

(The front cover photo shows the author connecting the helicopter sling hook to the Moke body ready for transport.)

An hour later I waved goodbye to the last sling load being the mini-moke body rapidly becoming a small dot on the horizon. I then retired to the pub, all agreeing this was a good day's work well done. About one hour later, on my fourth Bundy and coke, yet again I was called to the pub reception desk to answer the phone... it was Rinehart.

'Niven it is Ramdor speaking, I have ze good news an't ze bad news for you.'

Feeling a little let down at Reinhardt's stiff German attitude I decided to hear the bad news first...

'Ze bad news is ze lift hook has snapped on ze helicopter sling, causing your new mini-moke to fall from a height of three hundred unt twenty one metres into ze Northern Territory... destroying ze vehicle beyond all practical repair.'

I was stumped speechless, was Reinhardt having a German joke with me, but wait there was the good news...

'Are you serious Reiny, if that's the bad news what the bloody hell's the good news then?'

'Have you ze pencil to take down some urgent information Niven?'

I asked the hotel reception if they would please loan me a pencil and paper.

'OK go ahead Reinhardt I have a pencil now.'

'Then write down zizs figures 15 point 07 degrees. Twenty-six minutes South and 129 point 7 degrees. Thirty-eight minutes east. Have you got all zat down?'

'Yes but what do all these numbers mean Reinhardt?'

'Niven zat iz ze good news for you, we know exactly where your mini-moke iz. Zat iz ze map co-ordinates of ze last known place in ze Northern Territory where your new mini-moke was last seen, you will need zis information for your insurance claim.'

Insurance claim I repeated, I could hardly believe my ears. An insurance claim... this was ridiculous. No insurance company will pay-out on a vehicle; correction, "part of a vehicle" lost while transporting the said vehicle by helicopter into another Australian state, and lost from a height... no altitude of 1000 feet.

'I can't believe this Reinhardt. Are you serious about this vehicle loss? This must be some sort of German joke. You must understand that no insurance company will ever cover this type of loss. Anyway you have signed to accept all responsibility for any damage to this hire vehicle.'

Reinhardt Ramdor's answer was as swift to the point, and as unconvincing as was his solid German logic.

'Niven I do not make ze joke, ze vehicle was not completely delivered to ze working site an't was in ze care, and ze control of another person; to name Vowell

Air-services. This is not an Aquitaine responsibility. You must understand, ze lifting hook broke v'itch was not the fault of Aquitaine.'

This logic was most confusing to follow, just what the hell was Reinhardt up to saying stuff like that? Then Rinehart spoke again...

'I will be in mine office tomorrow morning at 5am sharp, you will come and inspect ze faulty hook an't see zis for yourself... goodbye Niven.'

The phone went dead with a loud click. Rinehart had said his piece. What a mess, how the hell Reinhardt could think my insurance company would pay for any of this was a mystery to me.

The next day I was in Reinhardt's office at 5am on the dot, I politely knocked on the office door, a voice from within commanded.

"Komminze Niven.'

Entering Reinhardt's office was like entering another world. It was full of mining, and drilling equipment of all kinds stored around the walls and floor. Leaning against the walls were piles of books, documents, and files all over the place. Everything was a mess except.... Reinhardt's desk, it was spotless. Polished and tidy with everything in its place including a large quality made, metal cast hook... with approximately one third of the tip part missing.

'See, inspect for yourself Niven. You will agree zat zis hook is faulty.

I picked up the cast hook out of curiosity and examined it carefully. This hook obviously made to a very high quality befitting of anything used on an aircraft. The safety lock was in place, but the hook was missing the end one third, making the lock useless. A closer inspection revealed that the casting had a large air bubble at the break line, providing an obvious casting fault in its manufacture.

Reinhardt looked on as I examined the hook with a blank, poker expressionless face… then added.

'You see what I am saying, ze hook iz faulty.'

This was amazing; that fault must have been in the lift hook from the time it was first cast. I then started thinking about all the helicopter lifts that went directly over the top of my house. And over the town, to supply the bricks and wet concrete to build the new ABC building and radio tower up on top of Kelly's Knob.

Then I remembered all the fooling around we did when the MD500 chopper first lifted the mini-moke. We all took turns at being photographed standing underneath the suspended Moke with our hands up pretending to hold the Moke up. This would have been just some ten minutes prior to the hook breaking on that last journey out to the drilling rig site. I snapped out of my frightening thoughts...

'Reinhardt, this is a problem not of my doing or responsibility. I will send you a bill for the cost of replacing the mini-moke, and the hire cost to date. I expect you to honour our agreement, and to accept all responsibility for the loss of my vehicle.

Might I suggest that you claim the costs from Vowell Air-services, who would no doubt in turn claim for their loss, from the suppliers and manufacturers of this very special, approved, and certified helicopter cargo hook?'

Reinhardt would make a good poker player as with a facial expression of hard stone he replied.

'Tender ze account if you vish Niven, but it will not be paid. Should you think so, you must take legal advice unt action on zis matter.' Then Reinhardt held a stern gaze, carefully adding. 'Any further conversation on zis matter must now be in writing for our solicitors to deal with... I bid you good day.'

My jaw must have been in the fully dropped position at this statement, Reinhardt then stood up from his desk, displaying the obvious signal that this meeting was now over... did I hear the click of heels? He had made his position clear, firmly believing that neither he nor his company Aquitaine were responsible for the loss of my hire vehicle.

Pursuing this matter through the legal system would have been a total waste of time and money, especially going up against a corporate giant such as Elf Aquitaine. There had to be a better way... and there was.

I wrote a passionate letter of understanding to the Australian head office of Elf Aquitaine in Melbourne, giving a full and detailed report on the problem vehicle hire. I was most surprised to receive a letter almost by return mail.

The letter confirmed that Elf Aquitaine would take full responsibility for the loss of the vehicle, and to expect the Australian general manager for Elf

Aquitaine to arrive in Kununurra within the next few weeks. He would like to pay the account in person with a company cheque, and that they would keep me informed.

A week later I received a phone call from the general manager. He advised me that his office was still in stitches with laughter over how this mini-moke was lost. They apologised that he would not be able to come to Kununurra for some months, but reassured me that they would cover all costs for the loss.

Well it was in fact some seven months before I finally received my cheque for the lost moke as promised, and it was as promised paid in person from the GM of Elf Aquitaine Australia. At the same time I also tendered the account for the mini-moke hire... all seven months of it, and to my delight and surprise, the account promptly paid in full.

About a month after Reinhardt had advised me that he was not going to pay, or take any responsibility for the mini-moke, he then transferred out of Kununurra to another urgent job. Denis Bosquet assured me that the transfer had nothing to do with my unfortunate vehicle loss, as this cost to Aquitaine considered as very small indeed.

I was advised the cost was just "a drop in the French ocean" compared with the daily funding and running costs of the Aquitaine drilling programme.

Denis Bosquet relayed this valuable information to me in a frustrating meeting down the pub. Denis was now expected to manage the complete Elf Aquitaine drilling programme, along with his Foraco drilling programme, until the company could find a replacement operations manager for Reinhardt. This only left me wondering one thing… just where the hell in the world was the French ocean?

Denis was at his wits end trying to manage and run his own Foraco drilling programme, and now supervising Aquitaine.

On top of all that, he had just recently slipped a disc in his back lifting heavy drill rods, and was in great pain. However, Denis had thought up a magnificent original French solution to ease this terrible pain in his back. A solution that included me, advising I could be of great help in resolving his painful back problem.

Chapter Seven

I want a red Mini Moke

That last story has reminded me of another Mini Moke story. You know, Mokes are special vehicles. This small vehicle was originally designed and built in 1959 by the British Motor Corporation (BMC.) Being a prototype for a light military vehicle, along the style of a field disposable American Willys Jeep.

It was not surprising, the military were not impressed with the small ten inch wheels, low ground clearance, and vulnerable alloy engine sump full of gears and other things.

The fact that it was very light, could be carried by four stout soldiers if it got bogged, and that it was cheap did not deter the British military from dumping the idea of buying this vehicle. It was deemed as unsuitable.

By the way, did you know that the name Moke was a slang-word for Donkey? Also an uneducated arsehole redneck. The one I like is the Moke reference to a water-pipe bowl full of marijuana… well so they say. This could well be the very reason for the strong British rejection. Sir Alec Issigonis has a lot to answer for in choosing this rather odd name.

By the early sixties British Leyland had all but given up in their attempt to get the military interested in the now renamed Leyland Moke. However the constant media and open attempts, attracted other interested people… The Moke was eventually released to the general public as a light fun vehicle, and soon became a cult must have set of wheels.

Hang in there, I promise you this story gets far more interesting… and funny.

In Australia the Mini Moke had found its true home. The light open top, simple and cheap vehicle becoming a favourite. Mokes were seen everywhere, used in a large range of outdoor activities; beach worshiper's, family second car, and as a trade's work vehicle. Soon the hire vehicle companies found this as an ideal choice, suitable for the Australian climate.

Over twenty six thousand Mokes were built and sold in Australia. This being the greatest number ever manufactured by any country in the world. Many Australian Mokes were exported, becoming a great little earner for the Land of Oz By far the largest sales of Mokes in Australia were made by the BMC/Leyland dealer Port Darwin Motors.

I first met Des Nudl (The owner of Port Darwin Motors) when I flew from Kununurra to Darwin to take delivery of three new Mokes to start my Vendal hire car business. The early model had small ten-inch wheels. Mokes were in Kununurra for some years; however, they performed poorly on unsealed roads. I noticed that some of the farmers had added Morris Minor fourteen inch wheels on the front raising the ground clearance. This fixed one problem but added a few others, unusable headlights and continually driving uphill to mention a few.

I ordered my three Mokes in 1973 shortly after Des Nudl had managed to convince Leyland Australia to modify the Australian made Mokes by installing thirteen inch wheels all round... This was the beginning of the first practical Mini Moke, a credit to Des and his brother Mick Nudl.

Over the following years, this order was only one of many vehicles purchased from Port Darwin. Des and his wife Dawn became close friends, and eventually godparents to our children Mark and Tracy.

The Moke hire business in Kununurra was to say the least, popular. It was the ideal vehicle to get around this small town and the surrounding area. At only eight dollars a day, they were cheap to hire. Later I was to think maybe too cheap, as any and everybody could afford to hire one... or two.

Why would anyone want to hire more than one Moke I hear you ask?

Well, I will tell you. One hot, dry day, I was in the Kununurra Hotel Cave bar, when I overheard three blokes talking about tonight's stock-car racing. What caught my ear was one bloke saying the only reason he was going, was to watch the Mini Moke racing. Adding the drivers were all bloody mad. The other bloke agreed with his mate saying the last race of the night, which had about twelve Mokes racing was the best.

I placed my rum and coke back on the bar giving me access to all my counting fingers. By my slick reckoning there were only seven privately owned Mokes in Kununurra, this left five other Mokes racing... whose were they? I figured this warranted an urgent first-hand investigation.

The Kununurra stock-car club was a popular club, holding racing events every Saturday night. Although me being in the automotive mechanical business, I was never a keen follower of the sport; however, all my workshop staff were. As were many other business people in town, I had done my bit having helped establish the venue. Through my electronics workshop, my main contribution was in providing and installing the track PA system, and other help. As such, I was an honorary club member, having total access to the venue at any time.

I arrived late at around ten, as I was only interested in the last Moke race. Making my way up to the commentary booth, I sat down in the dark behind the officials to watch the last race.

The racing was going well as the guys on the mikes whipped up excitement with the crowd. I was thinking

I should come to the racing more often, it looked like a good night out.

A glance out over the crowd. Bill was in the pits working on Morrie's car. Pedro, Gordon and Joe were in a good position in the front row, a little further along were two of the hire-car staff. All were having a good time.

Just then the PA bellowed out…

'Guys and Girls, we've come to our last event for his evening… The Moke demolition race. Get ready for the final Moke race of this season, called the demolition.'

The crowd roared with delight in anticipation of the pending wreckage and blood. A long line of Mini Mokes then drove out onto the race track with the drivers waving madly at the excited crowd.

I counted seven of my hire Mokes in the long line, one driven by my hire-car employee. Jumping to my feet I grabbed a microphone and began bellowing…

'This is Niven Dallas. All you shitheads driving my Vendal hire Mini Mokes get off the fucking race track. Your Moke hire contracts are in violation and are now cancelled.'

There was a brief silence as my demand was considered, then followed by a loud, angry, jeering, response from the well booze fuelled crowd of spectators.

'Fuck off Dallas. We've been watching your Mokes race every Saturday for the past ten weeks now.

This is the end-of-season finals, you can't stop this race now mate.'

The crowd roared in support of this piss-pot's request. That loud mouth remark came from the other side of the oval race track, so I could not identify just who this idiot was. Then one of the officials in the commentary booth stepped in with his two-bob worth of wisdom.

'Hang in there friends I'm sure that Dallas doesn't want to ruin tonight's fun. Just give me a minute to have a chat with him... Go have another drink while we sort this small problem out.'

I did not wait to have a chat with the race officials about giving my permission for racing to destruction my fleet of hire Mokes. Pulling the two other mikes out, I turned the PA amplifier up to full; then went about stating my case.

'My hire vehicles are not intended or covered by insurance for sporting events. If my vehicles are not removed from this race track, I will call on the attending Police officers to carry out this request as the hire vehicles are being used illegally.

Now I don't want to be a spoil-sport, and have a better suggestion I know you will all like.'

The crowd subdued down to hear my proposal.

'I have noticed a number of senior government managers in this crowd. I have also noticed that a large number of government vehicles are parked around the race track. I would like to suggest that this end-of-season race meeting should finish with an all government vehicle demolition race... what do you say?'

All the Moke vehicles had by now left the track, with the crowd applauding my suggestion. There followed a mass evacuation of the stock-car venue as the government people rushed to drive their government vehicles from the area. Now all I had to do was ask why all my staff thought racing the boss's hire fleet every Saturday night was a good idea... and just whose bloody idea was it anyway?

On the Monday I had a chat with the staff trying to work-out why they had thought it was a good idea to race my hire vehicles. Pedro said he didn't know anything about it (I know nothing.) Bill Gump had thought it was one of my brilliant advertising ideas, and I had obviously known all about it.

The others said something along the same lines, so I guessed this was going to be the cover-my-arse story... I was not going to gain anything from further poking around, so I closed the matter.

I called into my office, to have a chat with the hire car person who was about to drive my Moke in last Saturdays stock-car race. It was disappointing as she was really quite good at her job. But I had decided this was the last straw... she had to go.

My mind went back only a month when this same employee was involved in another Moke hire saga.

A hire client rang from Darwin requesting a Moke for an eight day hire. He would be arriving on the Darwin flight tomorrow and would like a red Moke. The red Moke hire was confirmed, a Vendal hire hostess would deliver his Moke to the airport and pick him up.

Apparently, things started to go wrong when the client noticed the Moke was yellow. After all, he had ordered a red Moke. He then became further irrational when told this was the only Moke available, and that he stunk of booze; to which he promptly replied that a silly flight hostess had spilt half a bottle of scotch down the front of him.

Things started to get silly again when the client said he was allergic to the colour yellow, and red was his best colour. Could we paint the Moke red for him? This same Moke racing hostess then advised the client she could not change the colour, to which the client said would she mind if he did. The hire hostess thought he was joking, and after all it was past six on a Friday night, replying it was okay by her.

Things started to happen rapidly after that. The next day I received a grumpy phone call from Frank, the owner of the Kununurra Hotel.

'Dallas there is a pissed-up bloke driving one of your Mokes in my front workers bar. He said it was his Moke but your name is on the side, so get over here and fuck him off. I have refused to serve him.'

I thought, did I hear right? "In his workers bar." It's only nine o'clock in the morning.

I jumped into my Toyota and drove over to the Hotel. Sure enough, there was my yellow Moke; driven through the double bar entry doors and up to the bar. Sitting on the bonnet were two skinny blokes leaning on the bar knocking back large cold beers. I let go of reality on witnessing this strange sight.

'What the fuck are you two doing?' then asking the client. 'Anyway, I thought Frank cut your booze off until you drove my Moke out of his workers bar?'

The bar manager looked on. Big Bad Betty with a smile on her face was busy polishing a beer glass, watching and listening. The answer was pure gold...

'Well here I is hanging out for a drink when I notices there ain't no bleeding bar stools to sit on in this pub. So I asks this good looking young lady here' pointing to Big Bad Betty, 'why there ain't no stools for a man to sit on. The lady then tells me the owner has removed them all cause they were used to fight with every night. I starts thinking of me bad back, then I figure the Moke bonnet is about the same height as a bar-stool, an just drives up to the bar.'

I thought to myself ingenious, I would have most probably done the same thing. Wanting to learn more I asked...

'What happened next?'

'Well, a few minutes later, this grumpy fat ding bloke comes up and tells me he is the owner of this fine establishment, and I won't get a drink until I reverse my Moke outa his workers bar. I told him there ain't no bloody bar stools to sit on mate. Then he just pissed off, an left me.'

I was fascinated, asking again…

'What happened next?'

'Another dry bloke came in. First thing he did was look for a stool to sit on. I told him there ain't any mate. Being a friendly kind-of-bloke myself, I offered him a seat at the bar. As a true gentleman, he kindly bought me a cold beer. And then you turns up. What can I do for you mate?'

Big Bad Bettys infectious smile was creeping across my face. We were both only a few seconds from all-out splitting laughter… then Frank arrived with a thunderous look wanting to know why this bloke was drinking at his bar.

I made my excuses and left. This was not my problem.

About a week later I got a phone call at around four in the afternoon from the Kununurra Police station. The sergeant informed me they had just received a call from the Northern Territory Police. Apparently they were holding a bloke in the Kathrine lock-up for being drunk and disorderly and driving a vehicle into a public bar. The bloke said he hired the red Moke in Kununurra, and he needed to return the vehicle today by six.

I told the local cops, even if the NT cops released him right now, he would never get back to Kununurra by six… it was a seven hour drive. Our local cops were experts at shuffling Police work, stating that the driver of my Moke had done nothing wrong in Western

Australia, and that was the extent of their jurisdiction. I added as an afterthought that the Moke in question was yellow, not red. The local Sergeant then gave me the direct unlisted phone number for the Kathrine NT Police. 'Ask for a Sergeant O'Malley'... I made the call, O'Malley's broad Irish accent answered my call.

'Katherine Police tis Sergeant O'Malley speaking.'

'Hi Sergeant, my name is Niven Dallas, I understand from the local Kununurra Police you have my yellow hire Moke and the driver...'

Before I could finish the sergeant interrupted me in full flow.

'Sir we don't hold that man now, he was released about half an hour ago. Another thing this Moke was red, are you sure this is the same vehicle sir?'

I was dumfounded... red, how could that be?

'And my Moke, where is my Mini Moke now?'

'We gave him his vehicle back. He had a signed contract stating he was the legal custodian. Apart from being held for ten hours for DD, tis man has committed no other offence sir.'

This was turning out to be a tricky business. So far everything this NT cop has said was correct, except for the colour. I should try another tact.

'Have you any idea where this bloke might have gone sergeant?'

'I tink I can help you there sir. To be sure he's gone straight back down to the pub. He was all of the shakes when he left here. I would say he was there now.'

I thanked the NT sergeant for his help and hung up the phone. I spent the rest of the day figuring how to get to Katherine, with no luck.

The only option was Aladdin Transport. Marko was a hard working truck freight operator, with a regular freight run between Kununurra and Darwin. Marko agreed to bring my Moke top loading on his way back from Darwin. He would be in Katherine at around five tomorrow, I should have the vehicle ready for him to load.

My next call was to Sergeant O'Malley in Katherine, it was now just before three. The idea was to advise the Sergeant that Aladdin Transport would be in Katherine in about two hours. Was my Moke still in Katherine, could he tell me where it might be? The Sergeant was quite jovial…

'Yor in luck me lad, I have the Moke and the driver locked in the holding cells as we speak.'

I thought about that for a moment… The Irish Policeman has locked my Moke in the holding cells with the driver? Surly this must be some sort of simple misunderstanding, I thought best not enquire along this line. Everything, no doubt will become clear in due course… asking…

'What was it this time sergeant, another DD charge?'

'Not quite' replied the happy Sergeant. 'We have added inciting a riot in a public place, engaging in animal blood sports with native animals, and illegal gambling.'

This had me intrigued, just what had this bloke been up too. In my evaluation of this bloke, he was just a happy, harmless piss-pot. The story the Sergeant told confirmed I should also add he was an idiot, and a top rated larrikin.

The Sergeant went on to say they had received an urgent call from the Katherine pub that a massive fight had broken out involving this bloke with the Moke. As the story goes, the Moke bloke overheard an old man in the pub tell about how ferocious his pet five foot Goanna was, and could kill any snake in less than a minute.

The Moke man challenged him to a bet for a cartoon of beer that his snake in the back of his Moke could kill the Goanna.

Soon the whole pub was taking bets on who would win. The Moke man went out and brought back an old flour sack with a huge snake in it.

He then went up to the old man at the bar, beat the sack several times against the bar and let out the biggest and meanest King Brown snake anyone had ever seen; right in front of the pet Goanna.

The bar panicked in all directions, but not before the spooked Goanna in fright ran up the side of its owner; clawing and ripping its way to the highest place and sat on the old man's Akubra…which was still on his head. Now with its claws dug deep into his skull.

Three other drinkers that were slow to get out of the Goannas way were badly mauled, as it ran across the top of the onlooking spectators.

Suddenly the Goanna realised in its slow brain, this was just another snake. It then came in with lightning speed for the kill. Five other drinkers in the bar were trampled in the rush to get out of the fighting pairs way. The hospital reported seventeen people were hurt in the ruckus, three quite badly.

The Goanna then ate the King Brown snake. I had assumed that the Moke man lost his bet. According to the sergeant it was a no win outcome for both, as the Goanna owner was going to spend quite some time in hospital; and the Moke man was going to spend quite some time in his jail.

My Moke was a mess. The pissed hirer had attempted to spray it red with a few cans of cheap paint spray. Kununurra Paint & Panel Works who carried out the repairs said he would never get a job with them.

I guess things could have turned out worse. At the very least I did get my Moke back in one piece.

I phoned Sergeant O'Malley again to thank him, but mainly to ask him a burning question. He must have read the hire contract, describing the Moke colour as yellow. Did he ask the driver why the vehicle was so poorly sprayed with red spray-pack paint? The sergeant agreed it was a bit odd, and said yes he did ask.

He replied that he ordered a red Moke, and was given a yellow one. When he complained, he was told he could paint the Moke any colour he liked. He liked red so he painted it red.

Chapter: Eight.

French lead poison

Almost all of the useful business in Kununurra normally carried out down at the pub. After all, the town was very small, and it was just as fast, and as quick to walk over and talk to the person in their office or the pub, as it was to talk on the phone.

The local pub then considered by many business people as the best, central, and most relaxed meeting place to sort out all the daily business problems. As such, that is what most business people did at the end of each long, busy day.

Denis thanked me again for suggesting Bill Gump as an employee. Foraco always had a problem keeping good staff on the drill-rig that were not French speaking, as few of his drill crew could speak a word of English.

For some reason with Bill, this did not seem to be a problem. As such he was pleased that he could send

Bill out to the various drill sites and the bush camp to work with his all French crew, but Denis was a worried man.

Over the last few months he was having an increasing social problem with his drill crew, there was an escalating level of violence among the drill-crew workers, arguments and fights were becoming an every-day event.

I glanced through the cave-bar and could see that Bill was having a drink in the other bar, and hoped that he would stay there for a while. I needed to finish my business chat with Denis, with drinks now in hand we continued our chat.

'Okay Denis hit me with it, this mighty plan of yours, but I must remind you of the last Aquitaine operations manager who had a brilliant idea. As you well know, that one cost me a new mini-moke.'

That remark got a wide smile on Denis's face helping him to forget his painful back for a moment.

'Ha Niv-an you are referring to le flying Moke incident no, that you will recall was a very German inspired plan, doomed to fail. My plan is all French, and is simple, and does not include any flying, or financial risk. I was going to suggest that you hire me one of your Holden sedan vehicles, which would have a softer ride and be better for my sore back; that is all, very simple no?'

I had to admit, it most certainly sounded like a simple plan, however it was no less a risk than Rinehart's great flying Moke solution. Although I could still see many major problems with this new French plan.

The first problem would be, that a car could not survive for long on the rough out-back dirt roads, on which this drilling company travelled for most of the time. Another thing that came to mind was the vehicle would, and without doubt, be used to carry everything, from bits of engines, to worn drilling heads, to down-hole drill samples. In short the car would end up as a total write off... in much the same way as the mini-moke ended up. These fears and my concerns were rapidly conveyed to Denis for his... French consideration and comment... Denis looked a bit miffed that his simple French solution not quickly embraced and accepted.

'Would it make any difference Niv-an, if I promised to look after le vehicle as if it were my very own?'

This offer came as a surprise knowing how Denis used and treated vehicles.

'Denis, your own family car is still out in the bush somewhere, broken-down. That's why Ida your lovely wife and your kid's have to walk to the shops in the heat. No Denis you won't convince me that looking after my car "like your very own" would be any comfort to me at all.'

Denis hunched his shoulders in the way the French do, saying. 'C'est la vie ' (such is life my friend).

I could see by the look on Denis's face that he was disappointed at my refusal to hire him a car. He had thought this was a good French workable plan to resolve his painful back problem.

I had over some considerable time, got to know Denis quite well. Denis would do anything to keep his drilling programme on track, and keep costs down. That would mean using all, and any available equipment, or resources, including my equipment, for whatever use to keep the Foraco and Aquitaine drilling programmes going. Then looking at Denis's painful face as he shifted his position at the bar to ease his back pain, I had a bright idea.

'Denis, I have thought up an all Australian plan you may wish to consider. I have noticed the Holden dealer in town has a nice new royal blue air-conditioned Kingswood V8 Utility on his showroom floor. If you can guarantee me a minimum of six months hire I will buy the bloody thing for you.

You would have to agree that only you and Ida to be the drivers, and because of the area of use; you would also have to take full responsibility for any damages to the vehicle.'

A glimmer of hope replaced the look of pain, then widened into a smile.

'Merci beaucoup (thank you very much) Niv-an I agree to your terms and promise to look after this vehicle as if it were my own.... err, maybe better than my own... no?

'Well I would certainly hope so Denis, I will purchase the Ute tomorrow and have it fitted with a bull-bar, tow-bar, and tinted windows for you.'

Just then Bill walked up to the bar. I must admit he looked much better than he did six weeks ago. I could still see the last lingering remains of his black eyes, and he now sported two perfectly spaced scars on his forehead, with his new little goatee beard he looked a bit satanic. Then a wide evil grin added the missing link, completing the look of the Devil. I thought to myself, no wonder the French drilling blokes did not bother him much, they were most likely shit scared of him. Bill then launched into an out-of-character, happy-chappie conversation.

'Hi there, now that's a bit of luck, both of my boss's in the bar to buy me a drink. I'll have a double Bundy and coke thank you.'

Bill was not backward in coming forward when it came to sponging a drink or two. Then again, he was always a lot happier after having consumed a few rum drinks. Bill had just arrived in from the Ningbing Foraco drill camp, and Denis was trying to extract a social report out of him, on what may be the latest problem out there.

'Tell me Monsieur Bill, how are the workers at the camp now that I 'ave reduced their beer and wine supplies, as the fighting quietened down any?'

Bill with a glint in his eye licked his lips in expectation as he picked up the Bundy and coke, took a long sip, and replied matter-of-factly.

'Well, since you asked me, I think they are a lot bloody worse. The cops were out there last night. That big frog bastard Pierre, he got stabbed in the arse by the little fat cook Louie. I don't know what it was all about, as I couldn't understand a bloody word they were both screaming mad about, but there was a hell-of-a lot blood everywhere.'

Denis's eyes shot wide open, he could not contain his surprise at Bill's more than casual statement.

'Sacré bleu, the Police you say, how did they know something was wrong at le camp, it is over two hour's rough drive from le town?'

Bill took another long drink, savouring both the rum and the moment of drama, adding…

'Well from what I could figure out, the cops were already on their way out to sort out last week's knife stabbing, and just timed it right for this week's arse stabbing. Anyway they all went back into town with the cops. Pierre had to get his slashed arse stitched up and the last I saw of Louie the cook, he had hand-cuffs on his wrists and ankles, and he was bloody fighting mad. This all happened about lunchtime; I thought you knew all about it boss.'

Denis was now looking a bit worried, then picking up his change from the bar...

'No I left le camp earlier, I must get over to the Police station and the hospital, if nothing else they will require a French interpreter, none of my crew can speak a word of English.'

As Denis left the bar at almost a run, Bill cried out after him.

'Yeh tell me about it, I just spent the last bleeding three weeks out there talking to those frog bastards with nothing but hand signals.'

This just left Bill and me at the bar, now would be an ideal time to get some background on what the hell is going on out at the Foraco drilling camp.

Bill was a sort of mechanical fix-it man for both the French drilling companies. He went out to both drill-camp locations Foraco and Aquitaine; as such he had met-up with all the crews. Bill by far preferred the Foraco camp, mainly because of its fixed location, and was much more established.

The road to the camp was better and only two hours drive from town. It was also very easy to find on the vast featureless Ningbing tidal flats, which stretch for many hundreds of kilometres. The camp easily found, being set-up at the base of a large rock outcrop that could be seen from a great distance. I started to quiz Bill...

'Tell me Bill; are the French blokes on the Aquitaine rig just as mad and knife happy as the Foraco blokes?'

'No bloody way.' Bill replied as he launched into his second Bundy and Coke. 'The Aquitaine crew are bloody angels compared with the mad Foraco blokes. I tell you if the Aquitaine crew were in the Foraco camp it would be perfect.'

This all sounded very strange to me. I had met many of the French drill crews at the pub and thought they were just a bunch of young guys, letting off steam, and having fun in laid back Australia. Then again I had noticed of late that Denis much preferred to keep the Foraco crew out at the camp, his reason was the

111

increasing arguments and incidents. Denis had put this behaviour down to the stressful drilling programme.

I had some doubts on this theory as the Aquitaine crew were under a far greater pressure to find a commercial oil strike, and they all got along very well. Another thing, Denis was having doubts himself since he was now managing both drilling programmes, and could see that the crews had a very different social behaviour.

I thought I would change the subject and asked Bill what he actually did each day. Moreover, what the hell was Foraco drilling for out at Ningbing as the Aquitaine "big rig" was now drilling in the Northern Territory, over 300 kilometres away?

Bill was staring at his empty glass, and I knew that I would not get an answer until he was well lubricated again, and so I ordered another two Bundy and cokes, and then Bill continued.

'The little Foraco rig drills between four or six holes a day, mostly in a line spaced about three hundred metres apart. That's a lot of work for a little drill-rig and the bloody thing keeps breaking down all the time, but conditions are getting better.'

'How's that Bill?'

'Well the rig and crew always stay out on site, but now the crew can come into the camp each night. That's because of the drilling programme, and sample results, which are bringing the rig closer and closer to the camp with each days drilling.

Give it another few days and we will be able to see the rig from the bloody camp, maybe I'll just walk to work next week.' This silly self-observation brought about a fit of chuckling into his Bundy, Bill laughing at his own joke... I used the unguarded moment to strike.

'And what are they drilling for Bill?'

I asked knowing full well that he would have been under strict instructions, and the threat of death to say nothing to anybody about French business.

'Buggered if I know,' replied Bill with a one shoulder hunch, 'but the samples look like this.'

Then reaching into his pocket he produced a lump of rock and placed it on the bar. It was dark in colour, almost black but with nice sparkly flecks of silver dotted through it. I picked the rock up and was surprised at the weight for its small size, then feeling the humourist I announced...

'Ah-ha, le French have found black gold in them their hills.'

Then placing the rock in my pocket I then let Bill know that I must leave his fabulous company. As I had urgent business to attend to in buying his boss a new Holden Ute to help with his bad back pain.

The Holden dealer starts business at 7am and I was there waiting, first thing as the doors opened. John File the parts man always opened up, and had the same view of me as the Holden dealer owner had, and that wasn't much.

In some way I could understand their reasoning. My vehicle hire fleet mainly consisted of locally purchased Toyota Land Cruisers and Hilux Utes owned by me. However, my Holden vehicles were always supplied to me by road or sea-freight; sent directly from Letz rent-a-car in Perth. Yet any required warranty service, or mechanical problems with my new Holden hire vehicles, now expected to be resolved by the local Holden dealer.

The dealer believed, and quite rightly so, that they were being used. Therefore, it was quite a surprise when I swooned into the Holden dealership, following John File up to the service counter. I then whipped out my chequebook, and filled in a cheque for the figure advertised on the windscreen of the shiny new royal blue V8 Ute on the display room floor.

The Ute was already fitted with a bull-bar and tow-bar, so on handing over the cheque I asked only for window tinting, and could he have the vehicle ready and registered by midday today. As I climbed back into my Toyota, I could see John still holding the cheque in his right hand with a stunned look on his face. I should have brought my camera.

Denis was full of gratitude while signing up for his new means of soft, back-saving transport. This was probably another time I should have taken a photo, a photo of my new Ute, because new hire vehicles don't look new for very long in the bush... as I was soon to find out only a few weeks later.

We had a quick drink in my office to celebrate the auspicious hand-over occasion. I remembered his last words as he drove out of the hire yard with a huge smile on his face...

'Niv-an 'av no worries mate, I will look after this beautiful machine for you, trust me.'

A few days later I was hiring a Toyota to a geologist from Sydney who was about to embark on yet another top-secret mission into the bush, when the thought struck me. I wonder if this geo could identify Bill's mysterious Foraco rock. I rummaged around in my office and found the rock in an ashtray on my desk.

The geologist examined the rock, pulling out a small eye magnifier to study it in detail. He then spat on the rock and rubbed it with his finger asking where I found the rock.

I am sure he was expecting me to name some bush location, but lost interest when I said I found it in the back of one of my hire vehicles. Handing the rock back, the geo said it was in his opinion a very high quality sample of silver lead. Could l tell him the name of the company who had been the hirer of the vehicle in which the sample found?

I told the geo this was not possible as all such client information was strictly confidential, and only on a need to know basis only. The geo told me that he did need to know, and I told him that I didn't need to tell him, so we left it at that.

This childish exchange of words, and the more than obvious interest in this rock convinced me that something big and important was going on out at Ningbing, my theory was later proved to be correct.

About a week later there was a buzz of gossip around the town pub. There had been a murder out at the Foraco camp, and someone was dead, stabbed to death in a fight. I had seen the blue Ute driving around so I knew Denis was back in town. I also found out that the mines department at the courthouse had been busy over the last few days processing a large number of mining tenement claims.

A phone call to Denis went ignored so I called in at his office. His office girl told me he was up at the Police station, after which he would most likely go the pub, so that's where I headed.

I noticed that Bill was in the workers bar, and I waved him to come across to the cave bar. I needed to tell him some good news that I was now ready to offer him a full-time job as a mechanic. This would also be a good opportunity to pump him for any information on the Foraco stabbing.

'Hi Bill haven't seen you for a few weeks what's all this about some Frenchman getting knifed to death out at the Foraco camp last night?'

Bill was surveying the bar top, then I realised that he was looking for a drink...

'The drinks are on the way Bill I just got here myself, well what happened out at the Foraco camp?'

Bill plonked himself down on the bar-stool looking his usual sad and glum self, he was not happy again. Maybe I should tell him about the job offer first, then before I could start talking he launched into an angry but interesting story.

'They're all fucking mad out there; I've told them all they can stick their job up their arse. You know that I really needed that job, but I reckon it's better to piss-off now than hang around to get stuck with some mad frogs bleeding knife.'

I could tell that Bill was really upset, more so by the capitulation of his job, a smart decision on Bill's part. He sadly continued his story.

'They all had a bloody big party out there last night to celebrate that the company had just discovered one of the world's richest silver-lead mines. You won't believe it, the stupid fuckers were camped right on top of the main silver-lead outcrop, that's what that bloody great rock outcrop was... it was made of solid bloody silver-lead. The stupid bastards were camped for months right on top of what they were looking for.'

This was amazing; I just couldn't believe my ears as my brain was working overtime on this news. The Bundy and cokes arrived just in time to settle Bill's anger down a bit. We both drank in silence, deep in thought. Just then a voice from behind me said.

'I will have one of those Bundy's too,' it was Denis; turning to face him, he must have read the questioning look on my face.

'I know you must 'ave heard Niv-an,' glancing at Bill, 'but owever, I cannot make a comment on le problem at the camp. Our French embassy is now andling this matter. Both peoples involved have gone to Darwin on the aircraft with a Policeman that is all I can say.'

'Denis, I won't ask you anything about last night's unfortunate problems, on the other hand, I may be able to shed some light on why things have turned out the way they have. Also I would like to suggest a possible explanation for the strange violent reaction by your French bloke who was involved in the knife fight, and now on his way to Darwin Casuarina prison.'

The look on Denis's face was that of defeat. He thought his French crew had brought shame and disgrace on the French name, this being a very serious matter to a Frenchman.

The French are among the proudest of nations in the world. After consuming more than enough drinks, Denis and I would often debate for many hours the successes of the French. Being world leaders in areas such as, seducing woman, the success of French cooking, inventing a way to remove one's head, the creation the bikini, and of course the giggle bubble drink… Champaign.

Denis would point out that it was the French who invented the bayonet. I on the other hand advised him that it was the British who improved the bayonet design, to fix the bloody thing over the mussel of a musket, and not in the end of the bloody mussel of the barrel. Thus the gun could still be fired with the bayonet in the fixed position… now how smart was that British idea… eh?

Although we defended our heritage, we never ever once discussed the detailed outcomes of the French in battle with the British. Out of 123 battles fought between 1743 to 1815 history shows French won 60 victories, and the British won 63. As for the odd three, well we just decided to have a drink on that, in the true Australian style...

'Tell me something Denis, your Ningbing camp, how did you provide the camp with potable water?'

The very tired looking Denis took a long sip of his drink, and stared into his glass.

'Like all drilling companies do I suppose? First we pick a likely spot for the camp site, and then second we drill a water bore to decide if the camp site is suitable. I will keep on test drilling until I get a good water-flow bore.'

'Denis, do you carry out any testing of the water quality; because my guess is the water in your Ningbing camp site water bore is dangerously high in lead content?'

The look on Denis's face took on a different and quizzical change, as the now obvious situation made crystal clear. His entire Foraco French drilling crew were all suffering from ingested lead poisoning?

The adult symptoms of lead poisoning include acute personality changes, memory loss, irritability, and inability to concentrate; this could explain everything that has happened out at the camp over the past six months.

'You should get the water bore sample tested, and also get the guys who are on their way to Darwin blood tested for lead levels. I think you will find this may well be the answer to all the problems experienced out at the Foraco Ningbing camp. Possibly offering an acceptable reason for the recent unusual violent behaviour, it may not be your drill crew's fault after all.'

I must confess this was still just my theory as to why the French Foraco drilling crew all went mad.

However, looking at Denis leaning on the bar to ease his back pain, I had the distinct feeling that he had already figured all this out, and was taking the (I say nothing) approach.

This murder matter was now well beyond a small-town local problem fixing. Being a large French national Company operating in Australia, this created yet another level of government problems, problems now sorted by their respective officials and bureaucrats. I think Denis was surprised that I had it all figured out, me being just a bush businessman of limited worldly knowledge... but why was he being so cautious?

Bill suddenly came alive after listening to all this and blurted out,

'With all these troubles and a murder out at the camp, the cops might throw Foraco out of the bloody Kimberley... no maybe out of Australia ha ha ha.'

This insensitive comment went down like a lead balloon (excuse the lead pun) with Denis who was now glaring at Bill's surprised face as he realised what he had just said. Bill had obviously been in the pub a lot longer than I had thought; Bill then quickly decided to go on to the defensive...

'I'm sorry about all the trouble out at the camp Denis, but I've bloody-well had enough, like I said out at the camp last night I want to quit my job with Foraco today.'

Listening to Bill speak, maybe Bill did ingest a toxic level of lead while out at the camp. I quickly dismissed this theory as Bill only drank rum and coke.

However, it was now more than obvious to both Denis and I, that the murder had affected Bill. Bill had reached his limit over this last incident.

There was just so much stress that Bill could handle. However, for me it was also interesting to note that both Bill and Denis were out at the camp party last night, and yet there was still fighting and violence. Denis may well be prevented from telling me the full story of what happened last night, but with a little more Bundy lubrication, Bill will eventually tell me all.

With a sympathetic look Denis turned to Bill...

'You 'av been a good mechanic Bill, and 'av put up with a lot of mad Frenchmen. I cannot blame you for this decision, 'owever we now 'av orders to finish the Foraco programme and bring in all the equipment's from the bush. Foraco will be moving out of the Kimberley, possibly Australia; our job in the Kimberley is all finished.

We 'av stopped drilling, and will be going home soon; this procedure will take about two weeks. Bill I ask you, will you stay long enough to help me dismantle the camp and equipment's, then bring everything into the town office yard?'

Chapter: Nine.

Australian Bastille Day

This news hit me like a brick. Maybe Bill was right about the cops showing Foraco the door, and then thinking back, Denis didn't mentioned anything about the silver-lead find. He must know all about this new discovery. Who the hell was going to develop the silver-lead mine, if indeed they were going to have a mine? And what about Aquitaine, who was going to run that massive drilling programme?

There were many questions, and if asked, would Denis answer any of them. Denis was enjoying this moment of mystery and speculation he had created by throwing those hand grenades into the conversation. He was obviously expecting a rush of questions from me... well he can wait, then turning to Bill...

'Bill can I suggest that you continue working for Denis until he has his Foraco camp sorted out, then when you have finished there, you can come and work for me... full-time at Multi Agencies.'

I backed away quickly as Bill tried to kiss me. I concluded this was a show of gratitude, I hoped not affection. This was a dream for Bill, as he would now be working with his best friend Peter again, and on light vehicles. Maybe not flash Rolls Royce motor cars, but certainly better than heavy diesel trucks. Bill immediately agreed to the idea, he would help Denis to dismantle the Foraco camp. I suggested to Bill that he ought to show his gratitude a mite by buying a round of drinks, and not kissing his new boss.

Two weeks passed quickly during which time I had only one quick meeting with Denis, who was flat out winding up the Foraco business. Denis confirmed that all the crew did test positive for high levels of lead poisoning. He was hoping with this new evidence the Police charges against some of his crew members might be dropped.

It was now mid-November, the start of the monsoon season again. The Foraco camp site decommissioning was taking much longer than first thought because of the early monsoon rains bogging down the trucks. Nevertheless, every day mud covered trucks loaded with Foraco equipment came into town.

Most of the French drill crew had flown back home, no doubt looking forward to a traditional cold French Christmas with their families. On the other hand, the town of Kununurra will never forget the drilling frogs, and the farewell parties at the Hotel

Kununurra pub. At every French party, all present had to learn the "La Marseillaise," the French national anthem.

I remember going down to the pub with Pedro for a quiet end-of-a-hard days drink. On getting out of the Ute we heard the loud renderings of the French national anthem. Pedro reckoned by the sound there must be all of the French drilling crew's in town tonight. We then headed for the cave-bar lounge as most of the noise was coming from that area. Entering the lounge, the singing was so loud, everybody was having a go at singing, the town Baker, the three Greek amigo painters, black fellers, white fellers, old wrinkled stockmen and even the bar staff.

They were all singing in very loud, very bad French. On the mini-stage at the back of the room stood four very tough looking French drillers, who I knew for a fact, could not speak a word of English. They were swinging their beers and drinking in time with the music with one hand, and conducting the pub patrons with the other.

These tough French drillers had managed to teach a pub full of new-Australians from all around the world, none of whom could speak a word of French to sing "La Marseillaise." My eyes and ears couldn't believe it, but it did turn out to be a good night at the pub. This was a firm reminder to me that Australia is a true multicultural country, and the laid-back, Australian way of life is by far the best culture in the world. All of this French hospitality reminded me of another very French occasion.

A few months back Denis and Ida had invited Lesley and I to celebrate Bastille day at their house. We arrived at about 7pm to a large party in full swing, and by the look of it, half the town was at Denis's Bastille Day party, there must have been over 150 people. The whole front-yard was a mass of coloured lights, French music, and people talking loudly.

I was thinking as Lesley and I arrived at the house, this is a lot of people to feed. Denis greeted us with a special Bastille Day drink called "blood and guts," but later revealed that it was just a potent fruit and tomato punch. We were then dragged off to his back-yard to inspect his latest creation, a newly built, all French designed brick bar-b-cue.

We had joined a small group of other admirers who were in deep discussion about its unusual architecture. Lucky for Denis we were standing at the back of this group as some of the comments were not very complimentary. The construction was remarkably different from the way a normal Australian bar-b-cue was built. The front sported a not-so-well-formed arc of bricks with a steel grid plate imbedded about halfway, another lower grid of steel supported a well-lit fire.

The Italian who owned an earth-moving company reckoned it was a very poor French attempt at building an Italian pizza oven. Another said it was a frog cooker of some sort, and yet another who was a pilot, was sure it was a very sophisticated; and most likely highly secret French navigation aid.

I noticed the smile quickly slip from Denis's face, as he witnessed at first hand the derogatory comments about his newly built masterpiece. It was more than obvious to me, and the other guests that Denis had been testing the "blood and guts" all day, no doubt making sure it was an acceptable French brew.

I stepped to one side, giving our host some room to vent his French anger. It was about now he wished to demonstrate that he had been in Australia for some years, and had learnt the local lingo extremely well. This being an example of how he had learnt to verbally abuse other people, mainly Australians. However, listening to his mimicking of an Australian rapport, with his French accent, was absolutely side-splitting.

'You are all a load of bloody fucking ignorant Australians, and 'ave no sophistications or educated experiences of this world. Anybody who 'as travelled in the slightest, knows what le "Arc de Triomphe de l'Etoile" looks like. Et is the world's largest triumphal arch, built by Napoleon himself.'

One smart-ass guest nonchalantly responded to Denis's outburst, by advising all present that "Napoleon was most certainly dead, and had been for some time, and that he could not have possibly built this arched bar-b-cue in Denis's backyard."

A local Dutch builder said. "The structure was very poorly built, and most certainly did not conform to the existing local and State building code, as such; it would most certainly be condemned by the local

Council. He was also very concerned, as he did notice a few Councillors were at the party."

The normally dim Post Master announced loudly. "He doubted Napoleon would have been granted a tourist visa to come here anyway, as he would have been listed on the watch list as a wanted fugitive from the island of Saint Helena." Now that last comment got a wide smile from Denis, at least somebody in Australia knew something about French history.

I just had to top that last comment. Stroking my chin in what I hoped was a sophisticated scholarly look... I then carefully directed my constructive thoughts at the smiling but very drunk Denis.

'Denis I was thinking that your creation resembles more like the "Arc de Triomphe du Carrousel." Being the much smaller triumphal arch, which was built at the entry of Napoleon's Palace residence, the arch that looks up the Voie Triumphal towards the world's largest Arc de I'Etoile, would you not agree?'

This did it... Denis was most impressed. His excitement caused his French workers to ask what the hell all the laughter was about, Denis relayed what had been said and they all erupted in laughter and smiles, with big André blasting off a rapid line of heavy guttural Marseille French. Then Denis translated...

'The closest I can get to what André has said is...'

"The fucking Australians 'av only been pretending to be idiots for the last two years. Maybe they are not such an ignorant load of arsehole shit-heads after all.

Tonight we will show them some good French cuisine, and a true French Bastille day of hospitality."

There was much backslapping, sign language, and drinking. Then there was a loud announcement.

'La nourriture est servie.' (The food is served.)

Denis then advised that all, the food had been prepared and cooked by his French drilling crew, and that they had been at it all day. He added with pride that the food would be an all French cuisine, with a touch of Australian ingredients included for added flavour.

We were all required to line up in front of a makeshift kitchen, being a low steel table, on which four large cast-iron pots were bubbling away. Each sat on gas-fired heating ring, all powered by a huge propane gas cylinder. I was later to find out, that this was the very same cooking equipment used to prepare the meals out at the camp site, brought-in especially for this Bastille Day party.

Further along, another table was set up with a very large… no giant, stainless steel platter on which sat a massive cooked bird complete with the legs wrapped in silver foil. I had never seen a bird of such a size in my life, and wondered just where they could have obtained this bird. We had all assumed that it was a special French import for this very special occasion.

Further along was yet another table full of various cold salads and sauces. I must admit the food smelt great, and the display spread was most impressive.

Everybody was happy and joking about what was in the pots, as many had asked the obvious question answered by the proud French server... in French, with a cheery smile. The whole back-yard was a mass of coloured lights, loud French music, and people talking loudly drinking huge amounts of the Bastille blood and guts punch.

The Bastille Day party continued on. Everybody was becoming increasingly drunk and a bit pushier about what was in the first and second pots. Then demanding what-the-hell was the large bird they were all trying to eat, as it was well... rather tough, and it stank a bit. About this time Denis thought it appropriate to have the Chefs acknowledged for their magnificent culinary efforts. Walking over to the large group of smiling drunken Frenchmen Denis banged on the side of a metal bucket...

'Attentions, attentions peoples, now we should thank our most capable Chefs for this magnifque feast on this Bastille day.'

Much cheering and clapping did not hide the already suspicious minds of the pissed party people… just then a loud heckler of unknown origin drowned out the Denis culinary speech...

'What are we thanking the Chefs for, we don't even know what the hell we're bloody-well eating Denis?'

This time the French drill crew didn't need any interpretation as they knew very well what the party guests wanted to know, "que diable sommes-nous manger" (what the hell are we eating?) Denis smiling

130

as ever, and now standing on his metal bucket for an elevated effect, waving his arms about like windmills. Although very drunk, responded to the heckler in his quaint French accent,

'Well Mesdames et Messieurs,' (Ladies and Gentlemen.) Denis swept his arms in a graceful, but unsteady bowing motion. 'Responding to popular demand (hic) I am elected by my peoples to explain what you are all eating tonight. Mainly on account of I am the only sober Frenchman 'ear 'oo can speak your Australian language, (hic.) in fact I am the only Frenchman 'ere 'oo can speak your language drunk or sober.'

Another voice from the crowd yelled out.

'Stop crapping on Denis and get on with it, we've got two Doctors here standing by just waiting on what medication to give us.'

The crowd burst into laughter again then settled down a little, and then the friendly bantering noise gradually abated. Everybody was now very closely focused on Denis, watching and waiting to hear what he had to say about the terrible food.

'Le first pot was a creation of "bat ragout," we collected a number of your tasty fruit bats, le flying fox's 'anging around along the trees of the Ord river, and prepared them in a beautiful stew with added seasoning. You would all agree it was magnifque no.'

Everybody loudly disagreed with Denis, nobody thought it was magnificent at all. The bat stew was bloody awful, but these comments went right over Denis's drunken head. Somebody else yelled out.

'If I die here tonight from bat poisoning, I will personally haunt you as an angry ghost, and set my cranky dog on to you.'

Denis was by this time totally alcoholically insulated from any form of verbal abuse, and by all accounts not in the least deterred by this threatening guest. He then took a large swig of his Bastille blood and gut's punch, and then continued with his grand speech... addressing the last hecklers threat of a dog-attack.

'Prenez une belle maison Bastille de nourriture pour votre chien de mon ami) (Yes, do take home some of our beautiful Bastille bat food for your dog my friend.)

Now to le second pot of this beautiful selection, (hic) a casserole of specially prepared frogs leg's in red Bordeaux wine cooked to perfection by our drill-camp cook Maurice.'

Maurice the little plump cook, complete with a French beret on his head, came to Denis's side and took a deep bow of gratitude to the now jeering crowd of guests, one yelled out.

'I hope you bloody-well imported those fucking frogs from France Maurice?'

Denis was quick to reply, directly addressing the rude loudmouthed heckling person...

'No need worry Doctor Gordon (hic) my French crew 'av good experience in preparing le frogs and 'ave found plenty at Lilly Creek at le town road turn-off. I can tell you they are a much better size than back home. You know they are a special delicacy in Paris no.'

A stunned silence fell over the large group of Bastille guests, some of mutterings heard were.

'He's got to be fucking kidding, those bloody flying foxes have rabies don't they?' then other comments were.

'I bet you they don't eat our shitty green frogs in Paris restaurants... local Kununurra frogs eat mosquitoes and their lava, what about malaria?'

Then the local Police Sergeant stirred the crowd with a bit of sound Australian logic and common sense. By suggesting that if they were all going to die tonight of bat and frog poisoning, then they should at least finish off all the booze first. All unanimously accepted the Sergeants suggestion as the best idea. But I had another leading culinary question to ask...

'Denis, what the hell was the make of that bloody great bird we are all trying to eat?'

Denis had a quick chat with his little French Chef Maurice, and came back with a beaming smiling face. Then standing on his tin bucket again, but looking somewhat more unsteady...

'No problems my Bastille Day guests (hic) I 'av the answer from my French Chef's, you were all eating the great Australian delicacy. Bush Turkey, cooked to perfection... opp's,' as Denis fell off his tin bucket and landed in a heap on the ground, nobody came to help him up as all in the crowd had been stunned into total silence by this shattering admission.

Now the so-called Bush turkey is an Australian protected bird species. The Bustard bird or Ardeotis Australis as the learned ones prefer to call it. On the other hand most local people prefer to call it the Goony Bird. It's the most stupid and silliest big bird on the face of planet earth. It can fly, just about, but prefers to run away if frightened, after all it weighs over ten kilos. It has few if any natural enemies or predators, as they consider it is not worth eating because it tastes awful and is so tough.

The local indigenous people, the Aboriginals, will only eat one as a very last dying resort to survive starvation. They have over the years tried to palm them off onto unsuspecting whitefella by calling them "Bush Turkeys." As I was later to find out, the French drill crew accidentally ran over one the day before, and decided to cook it up as a special treat for Bastille Day.

All the Bastille Day guests thought the French had cooked the Bustard bird as a joke, and treated the event as just that... I on the other hand know for a fact that the big bird was to be the "piece de résistance" (best part, something special.) Maurice the French camp cook was not happy to hear the truth about this Goony Bird.

Nobody was impressed with the Bastille food; however, everybody reckoned the French Bastille Day celebration in Kununurra was one of the best parties ever held in the town. I had no problem in rating the event a four-out of five, four being the number of days my hangover lasted, and five being the number of days I had off work seeking rest and repair to my digestive system, and that of my overworked rectum... "C'est la vie" (that's life)

Chapter: Ten.

Sacré bleu a two piece Ute

Kununurra was winding down on the oil drilling business. There was noticeably less French drilling crew about town. Was this the lull before the storm or was this the end of yet another phase, I had seen it all before. We needed to plan for the next move.

Other things were happening; exploration companies were enquiring about the availability of 4X4 hire vehicles… I must keep my eye on the ball as I have eight weekly wages to find and a large bank overdraft to service. This called for an urgent management meeting as such advised Pedro we should have a drink at the pub to discuss important things about future work prospects.

As we pulled into the pub car park we could hear the loud singing… it was French, very bad French, yet another Foraco farewell party was in progress.

Pedro had returned from the bar with the drinks, while I was still in deep thoughts about the mad party on Bastille Day with these same French blokes that were on the pub stage.

I think the French nationals really did enjoy the Australian laid-back way of life, and no doubt will have some regrets at going back home. Then again they will all have some very interesting stories to tell their families and friends, like this one of teaching a pub full of Australians how to sing the French national anthem.

The cave-bar was becoming more crowded and noisy, so Pedro and I, seeking somewhere quieter decided to change bar locations to the workers bar. This was the domain of Big Bad Betty. BBB was the bar manager and ran this bar with a no nonsense iron fist. Being a rather large lady of about thirty odd years of age, BBB was a most experienced lady in the ways of men, mostly their bad ways, especially when they were blind drunk and in full fighting mood.

Large BBB may be, but she was every bit a lady, always with well-groomed hair and nice just enough make-up. This lady was well spoken, smarter than the average bar wench, a lady with a fast sharp tongue that could cut down any would-be smart-assed bar fool in a fraction of a second. She was most certainly not a woman to cross swords or words with at any level. Big Bad Betty had been known on occasions to break-up bar fights wielding two heavy glass handled beer jugs, as such was respected within the heavy drinking fraternity for many hundreds of kilometres around.

This was a busy time of the year for BBB as the cattle droving and mustering season had just ended. This would bring into town all the station drovers, ringers, Jillaroos and Jackaroos, all looking for a good time. The whole town looked like a scene from an old American wild-west movie. With stockmen clinking around in spurs strapped onto their RM Williams boots, dressed in their Australian stockman's gear, topped off with their sweaty Akubra hats and a self-rolled cigarette dripping out their mouths.

These tough station-hands were men and women of the bush, most had never had a drink in over six months, as many of the cattle stations in the bush were dry (no booze allowed.) They arrived into town with pockets full of money, mainly because they had nothing to spend their hard-earned money on out at the cattle station.

These station people were very special people indeed, and had a simple code of conduct, "Try to help someone who was down and in need." "Never see someone short of a feed or a drink," and "It's always best to forgive someone for what they did while they were drunk."

Big Bad Betty knew this code well. As such she was always on the lookout for the town bar-flies. The vultures and scavengers who would attempt take advantage of these hardworking cattle men and women, with their generous laid-back easy-going attitude and lifestyle.

Pedro and I pulled up a bar stool just as "Big Bad Betty" strolled up the length of bar to greet us with a big smile.

'Hi strangers don't see you guys in this bar much, can't say I blame you with all that French singing going on next door, what will you lads have.'

The workers bar was separated by the garden slide bar, going through to the cave-bar. BBB would have seen us almost every day, however, she rarely if ever served in the cave-bar, this was her bar, and she was the boss lady. I replied.

'Two Swan middies for a start please BBB.'

Glancing up to the top shelf behind the bar, I took note of BBB's now usual line of large clear-glass pickle jars. Each jar had a name on it Sam, Brumby, Little Horse, Johno, Ben, and so-on. Each jar held a large quantity of rolled-up paper money and coins... This was the Big Bad Betty Bank. I glanced up the length of the bar, and there sure enough was the very reason why. Drinkers at the bar had a small stash of money on the bar in front of them, this was the traditional Australian bar-drinkers way.

You ordered your drink, or round-of-drinks and the barmaid just took the money from your pile of cash on the bar. The only thing was, when you came to town with four or five thousand dollars and placed that on the bar, you soon attracted a large circle of new friends. As BBB would say, the bad element, the vultures and scavengers.

Now this brings me to how Big Bad Betty earned this auspicious name, well, I can make some rightful claim to that odd privilege.

One day down at the pub, a larger than normal group of station people were having a nice time drinking and trying very hard to be good. Unfortunately the scavengers were again out in force helping the Jackaroos and Jillaroos spend their hard-earned money, then one thoughtless fool stepped out-of-line a bit too far.

Betty had noticed out of the corner of her ever watchful eye. A well-known bar-fly of the lowest kind, was spotted helping himself to a station-hands bar money. The deed carried out while the ringer was off making room for yet more booze. Quick as a flash Betty stopped cleaning the large heavy glass beer-jug she was holding, bringing it down hard on the un-suspecting bar-fly's fingers, breaking four of them in the process.

Stealing a man's money, especially when that same man was buying you free booze is the lowest of any crime in the bush cattleman's crime-book, and as expected requires a response of the highest order. As a result the bar erupted into an almighty brawl. Betty realised that it was she who had drawn attention to this stealing matter and was ultimately to blame for the now ensuing bar brawl.

History records the event, as the very first time that Betty had taken-up her now famous "Twin jug" fighting role by firmly grasping another large beer jug.

Betty now had one jug in each hand, and then waged into the centre of the brawling mass of fighting ringers and station-hands. She went about breaking up the fight single-handed while all the other bar-staff were meekly looking on.

Nobody in his, or her right mind would ever hurt or lay a finger on Betty... that would have ended up as a murder in the bar. Everybody respected, and might I add, loved Betty. The bar soon returned to normal, and since the Police were never called or required, at this time the matter was resolved... That particular bar-fly was smart enough to never show his face in town again. The next day after hearing of this absolute act of total bravery by Betty, I ordered a drink from her... on delivering the drink the name sort of just slipped out...

'Thank you Big Bad Betty.'

The name stuck. BBB did not take any offence at the name. (Just as well) in fact, I do believe that this name may have helped to change the minds and attitudes of some of the newer young drinkers that later braced Betty's workers bar. Especially those that were smart enough to enquire first as to why the barmaid was called "Big Bad Betty."

Shortly after this money stealing episode, BBB decided to resolve the money temptation problem forever, by taking care of the visiting station-hands hard-earned money. BBB would take all but a few dollars of the station-hands money off them. She then and put the balance their cash into large glass pickle jars with the name of the owner on it for all to see. BBB would then refuse to be the banker for rounds for the bar, and other such extremes of needlessly throwing money around.

She would also cut off the owners own cash funds when they were drunk-as-a-skunk, and had had enough. She would also (in her own time) pay the ringers motel accommodation and food tab, and would also pay their town shopping from their money jar in the workers bar. Then when the ringer or station-hand was due to go back to the station, BBB would arrange the transport, and hand over any remaining cash to the station manager. Everyone loved Big Bad Betty.

The first beer went down well, a raging thirst now alleviated; it was now time for a Bundy-and-coke. Looking around the workers bar, there was some sad examples of worn-out old men, and even sadder, a few young alcoholics, both black-and-white.

Since Aboriginal drinking rights came into force in 1967, I had noticed the Aboriginal alcohol problem had dramatically increased. North-West hotels and pubs were full of pathetically drunk indigenous people, with free government cash handouts to pay the booze bill. These once proud people now gradually reduced to alcoholic human trash with the white-man's (whitefella) booze. The pub and booze was now their only way of life. I then remarked to Pedro.

'You know something Pete, could we end up just like that, what do you think went wrong in their lives. Do they have any caring family, is someone waiting somewhere and missing them? We must make sure this never happens in our lives.'

Pedro looked at the human wrecks then quickly looked away in disgust, nodding in agreement and quietly said.

'Let's get out of here Niv, all the normal happy people have gone next door to learn the French national anthem, all that's left here is the dregs of this world, it's depressing.'

I had to admit that I agreed. These miserable feelings required an urgent change of subject before we went into a spiralling mood of ever manic depression. Just as that morbid thought went through my mind, I caught sight of Bill Gump sitting on a bar stool, rum drink in hand, all alone in the cave-bar. He had his usual glum look on his face and not taking part in any of the singing, then turning to Pedro.

'How's Bill going in the workshop, I have noticed that he gets upset quite often and has a bit-of-a temper, I have seen him throw stuff around in the workshop and cursing. I would have thought he'd have been happy now working with you. What the hell's wrong with him?'

Pedro finished his drink and headed for the door. He had a grin on his face, so I knew he was about to say something amusing, we could do with a laugh after the workers bar. I decided to head for the outside beer garden; Pedro hunched his shoulders and began his story.

'Bill is a very good mechanic, I tell you there's nothing he can't fix, and even his paperwork is good. His job-cards filled out in immaculate detail with everything charged out. One thing though, I have noticed over time is that Bill might be good with mechanical things, but he is not so good with women.

Coupled with his normal manic depression, I think right now Bill is suffering a far greater mental stress, frustration. He can fix all sorts of mechanical stuff, but he can't fix his love-life. Put quite simply, he's never had a fuck... he's a bloody virgin.'

I must admit I was quite shocked, especially as that explanation was put... well, quite brutally by Pedro. I might also add, this is a huge problem that exists for just about every young red-blooded male in this very remote area; quite simply there were not enough available women in this small town.

Even the ugly women were having their pick of a large group of available male testosterone. Therefore, Bill, not being blessed in the good looks department, had some almighty fierce competition in the local female love stakes.

'You know Pedro, Bill seems to get into the wrong situation quite a lot, surely it can't all be just his bad luck. I mean putting aside his many car accidents for a moment, and taking this present situation of a loveless life. Bill must have known that if he couldn't get a fuck in the big city of Perth. Then his chances of getting laid in this sparsely populated remote area of the Kimberley would be almost impossible.'

Pedro ordered a round of drinks, and then a smile returned to his face,

'I warned Bill about that when he decided to follow me up here. He reckoned that if he couldn't get a fuck in Perth, then he wouldn't get a fuck anywhere and he might as well try getting a job in a Catholic Convent, as a celibate motor mechanic.'

This thought brought a grin to my face and broke our sombre mood. We sat-down under a nice shady tree in the beer garden to continue our pleasant drink, with the French singing still continuing in the background, and then another important question came to mind.

'Pedro, why do you think it is that Bill never suffered from lead poisoning like all the others did, after all he was out at the Foraco camp for weeks on end? He would have drunk from the same bore water, and had a swim in their homemade pool, filled with the same lead contaminated water?'

I could see my question had caught Pedro by surprise as he had just done his normal thing and hunched his shoulders… He then looked skywards for inspiration; I detected a spark of wisdom in his eyes as he formed an acceptable answer.

'I dunno Niv, but I have noticed that Bill never ever really gets drunk, yet he drinks more booze than anybody I know. The only difference is he goes from being his usual miserable self, to a happy chappie. Maybe his system just doesn't absorb alcoholic fluids like everybody else?

I thought about this for a second. I had also noticed this strange behaviour myself, Pedro was right, he should get drunk out of his mind just like all the rest of us. Then there was this other strange thing about Bill, he could handle a lot of pain extremely well. He was the clumsiest man I had ever known, and always sporting some sort of self-inflicted wound caused while working. However, none of it ever seemed to bother him, I gave my opinion.

'Bill Gump is a very complicated man Pedro. I have seen him spend all of his weekend helping people fix-up their stock cars and boats, he will give his time to help anybody, and he's a real nice guy. I think he wants the friendship more than anything else. The problem could be he's just a lonely man.'

Pedro took a sip from his beer, placing the heavy glass gently down on the table. He then took on a look of concerned seriousness, and revealed to me his inner thoughts, and what he thought to be the absolute truth.

'I think Bill is not from this Earth.' Then with a little chuckle, 'Well he doesn't act like an earthling. Maybe he's from Mars, or maybe his body has been invaded by… something…'

Hearing this, I delayed the glass an inch from my lips and replied in all sincerity.

'You mean, you think Bill might be some sort of... Alien?'

Pedro wiped the beer froth from his chin with the back of his hand and stared into my eyes. Noting my deep interest, he then continued with new enthusiasm.

'Well you think about it Niven. He doesn't feel any pain, we can't get him drunk, and he has this overwhelming desire to make babies... all the basic qualifications of an Alien if ever I've seen one.'

Pedro was of course perfectly correct. There was no doubting it now; Bill was obviously an Alien of some sort… a spy from another planet. Without saying another word we finished our drinks, got up from the table, and went home.

About a week later I had a phone call from Denis.

'Ah Niv-an I am back from le bush, everything is almost done I 'ave something important to tell you, can I come to your office?'

Suspicious, well yes I was... My suspicion was well founded; it was after all only a little after midday on a Monday, any such important meetings would normally be held at the second office... the town pub.

'Denis, I was halfway out the door, and late as usual for another urgent meeting. I must confess Denis it's another one of those (I want to see you here right now,) a meetings with the new Commonwealth Bank manager. Can I see you down the pub at about one' o'clock my French friend?'

It didn't take long for my newly arrived in Kununurra Bank manager to turn down my new loan application. No doubt a quick look at my personnel file had fully supported his easy decision. He then started politely crooning on about me having already exceeded my overdraft limit, advising this was a serious matter.

I tried in vain to explain to the man that this was the very reason I needed the damn loan. The puzzled look on the new Bank managers face told me he wasn't getting my drift, and that I wasn't getting the loan. I could tell this new bank manager needed more time in the job to absorb the normal Kimberley area, business banking style. As such, I was out of the bank in twenty minutes flat and heading for the pub.

As I pulled up out-side the Hotel so did one of the big Foraco drilling rig trucks, followed by the maintenance truck, and then the generator truck. This would only leave the water truck and the drill-rod truck to arrive for the complete Foraco drilling system.

They had all lined-up outside the Hotel on the wide road verge as there-was no way that they would find enough space in the car park. I could see that all the trucks were covered in thick grey Kimberley mud. It was obvious the trucks had been recently bogged up to their axles. I then noticed that the heavy steel towropes were just wrapped around the bull-bars and not winched back on their drums.

The crews had obviously made a beeline direct for the pub; it must have been hell out on the track in this heat, humidity, and mud. I was thinking to myself if they don't get that damn mud off soon it will dry rock-hard like concrete, so hard that even a powerful steam cleaner will have difficulty removing it.

Denis was already in the cave-bar surrounded by about twelve of his drill crew all chatting away in loud French. The conversation stopped dead when they noticed me approach.

"Allo Niv-an my friend I am 'appy to see you, I 'ope you will be 'appy to see me, what will you 'av to drink?'

By now I was very a suspicious man. Denis knows I drink Bundy-rum and coke, and what's this happy to see you bit? He only lives two doors down the road. All the French crew were looking at me with big grins on their faces. André the big roughneck driller kept saying to Denis "allez lui dire sur" which I later found out was (go on tell him)

'I'll have my usual rum and coke thanks. What's going on with this lot,' glancing at the group of grinning French drillers, and why are they all staring at me, turning again to Denis. 'Anyway what was it you wanted to tell me about so urgently?'

Denis took a deep breath and launched into his story...

'Niv-an I want to be the first to tell you about the important discovery we 'av made out at Ningbing. We 'av found one of the largest, and richest silver-lead deposits in the world. This will be good for this small-town and also for your business no.'

This was a strange opening from Denis... something was up, something was not right.

'Just hang on their Denis, I know all about the silver-lead deposit, your bloody drill-camp was built right on top of it, remember. That's how this lot,' waving my arms at the group of leering Frenchmen, 'all got bloody lead poisoning and went knife fighting mad.'

'Ah but Niv-an, what you don't know is there will be a full underground silver-lead mine in operations very soon, with a pelletising plant built on site. Many peoples will come for work at this mine and trucks will come and go many times a day to the Wyndham Port with the ore. This will bring much good business to the Town no.'

I was warming to this idea of a mine right on our doorstep. Yes I could see a big advantage for the Town, but suspicion still nagged at me. Denis could have told me all of this over the phone. I know Denis; he was hiding something else. Big André gave Denis another elbow in the side saying "pourquoi est-il toujours le sourire" which I later found out to be (why is he still smiling). I was standing with my back to the window looking at this group of suspicious guys, when the little fat cook Maurice gave out a gasp and his eyes opened up to saucer size.

The rest of the crew paused in their drinking and stared straight passed me with their mouths locked in a grin. Turning to see just what could possibly cause such an odd reaction, I was stunned into a frozen stupor, dropping my full rum and coke in the process.

Clearly visible through the large windows was the drill-pipe truck loaded to the maximum with a full load of drilling rods. Chained down firmly, on top of the drill-rod load, was my almost new blue V8 Holden Ute. The only problem was, the front-end being chained down as a separate bit to the rear end, at some twelve metres apart. The bloody thing was in two separate halves.

Only now could I understand why Denis had said (hope you will be happy to see me.) I was still in shock at this odd spectacle when a small worried voice from behind me said...

'I am so sorry Niv-an, we 'ad a little accident in le bush last night and your Ute was... well broken a little. I wanted to tell you about this in your office but my drill crew wanted to see your appy face, and that we managed to bring your Ute back to town.'

Denis quickly translated this to French and then the whole pub erupted in laughter. It was obvious the French drilling crew didn't care a rat's arse about my new Holden Ute. They just wanted to see what my reaction would be when I first set eyes on the remains of my new hire vehicle. After a few seconds I attempted to calm down and compose myself...

'What the fucking hell happened to my new hire car, you said you would look after this vehicle as if your own,' then looking Denis squarely in the eye. 'I was only trying to help you and your bloody bad back. Trying to do the right thing... this is not a joke, this is no laughing matter,' then using my few words of French.

'Saint merde amis, c'est terrible.' (Holy shit mates this is terrible)

Well that last comment when translated (as my French was not very good) just about brought the house down, the whole bar was twisted in raucous laughter, backslapping and whooping. I have to admit that I cracked under the pressure, joining them in the gut wrenching laughter. It was indeed a very funny thing for them, and a very sad day for my profits. Then as the minutes past I came to realised the funny side of all this, after all... what could I do.

Apparently, the problem started when the huge drilling rig truck became hopelessly bogged, travelling on the well-used and muddy road from the Foraco

Ningbing camp site. The drill-rod truck had also got stuck while attempting to pull drill-rig out. They were almost successful in their rescue task when Denis arrived on the scene, yes in his blue Holden Ute.

Both of these heavy trucks were still connected together by a thick, steel, towrope from the drill-rig's front winch. However, try as they may, the rod truck in combination with the drill-rig winch just couldn't quite pull the rig out. They were just about to unload the drill-rods to lighten-up the truck, when Louie the big roughneck came up with a brilliant and original French idea.

If the boss could just hook-up his blue Ute to the front of the rod truck this might be just enough grunt to do the trick. Things were looking good for a short while, but the winch on the drill-rig truck was just a little too powerful and dragged both the rod-truck and the Ute backwards. Just then the water-truck arrived on this scene and backed up to the Ute, a steel towrope then attached to the front of the Ute. About then the maintenance truck had also arrived, they decided that they might as well hook that up as well.

Now let me try paint the picture for you. Here we have four very large twenty ton mining company trucks all of which are four-wheel-drive vehicles fitted with powerful cable winches and powerful diesel engines fitted with reduction gearboxes. The line-up is as follows. The 4X4 drill-rig truck now connected to the 4X4 drill-rod truck, in turn connected to the towbar of my new blue Holden Ute. The front bull-bar of my new Ute then connected to the rear of the 4X4 water truck.

Then the last huge truck firmly connected to the 4X4 maintenance truck… got it.

Everything was ready, the signal was about to be made to start the pull when Maurice, the little fat cook shouted "arrêter" (STOP). He had noticed that the water truck was still full of water, suggesting that this would ruin the attempt because of the excessive weight. Without a moment's hesitation the water truck driver pulled a lever in his cab and discharged all 8000 litres of water out the rear of the tanker on to the already boggy road and under my new blue Holden Ute. With the heavy water load now discharged the mighty rescue tow resumed.

The two rear trucks started pulling in on their powerful winches to drag themselves forward, and the two front trucks started their tow in low gear 4X4 pull forwards... then it happened... yes it did indeed happen.

Big André with a wide grin and much waving of arms, bellowed out in loud French that hardly required any English translation,

'Niv-an "le maillon le plus faible a été premier mate" (the weakest link went first mate) ka-boom.'

My beautiful new blue Holden Ute ultimately torn apart with little effort, the break took place at the back of the cab, so the two parts consisted of the front wheels, bonnet, and cab, the second half being the rear axle, wheels, and the Ute body.

Denis no longer had a nice Holden Ute to get around in; then again, with the Foraco drilling programme coming to an end, would he still require such soft transport? A thought hit me, just who was going to run the huge Elf Aquitaine drilling programme? As I was carefully considering my next question about these important matters, Denis answered my very thoughts.

'We are all going across to Queensland to start a new drilling programme there with another crew, and with another operations manager. I will stay with the old drilling rig to finish logging all the holes we 'ave made. Maybe two weeks and then I will go to Brisbane to run the office... you will miss me no?'

'Yes Denis I will most certainly miss you, possibly more than my new Holden Ute, and I will also miss all the good times we, and our families have had over the last three and a half years you have been in Kununurra.'

'Niv-an do not worry about this vehicle I will pay you what it cost but the ute now belongs to me no, the ute will remain on the drill-rod truck and go with us to Queensland.'

'That sounds fair enough to me Denis. You now own the two halves of a blue Holden V8 Ute with less than 4000 kilometres on the clock.'

Denis and his rough-neck French drilling crew were grinning from ear-to-ear enjoying and savouring every minute of this hire vehicle tragedy. Denis continued still with a beaming grin and announced...

'Oh yes Niv-an, I must also tell you that a new general manager will be here next week to take over the operations of Elf Aquitaine, his name is Maurice Rowley.'

A few days later Lesley and I joined Denis and Ida for a private farewell dinner at the Hotel Kununurra.

We were sad to see the Bosquet family go, but such is the nature of exploration and drilling company personnel. Almost four years working in the Kimberley was a long drilling programme for Foraco. However, we still had the parent company Elf Aquitaine, at least for a while, the company now based in the Northern Territory; and still looking for oil.

Things were hotting up in the Kimberley. I had noticed that about five new major exploration-drilling companies had recently moved into this region, and oil was not on their list of interest.

There was new and valuable merchandise somewhere in this Kimberley area… the whisper on the mumble-vine was diamonds.

These new compact drill rigs were here to sample and test-drill for diamonds. Diamonds that they all knew are most certainly here, but just can't quite find the source at the moment, well time will tell. My guess is the mad Geologists and secret drilling programmes will soon be on again, this time looking for diamonds. In the meantime I still have a major problem looming with Mister Bill Gump.

Chapter: Eleven

Best effort to end it all

As the weeks flew by, the mechanical workshop and the 4X4 hire vehicles became much busier. An unexpected demand came from all the new diamond exploration companies now based in and around town.

With the increasing mechanical service workload, Bill was also becoming crankier by the day. I had thought that when Bill got his Leyland P76 back from the panel shop that would have made him a little happier, but this was not the case.

Many of the parts needed to complete the repairs were no longer available or now poorly made. Bill had to take the vehicle back from the panel shop with a number of small bits still missing like the windscreen surround bright trim, and the interior headlining.

He had three sets of these sent up and all were either cut too short or moulded to the wrong windscreen shape, many other urgently needed parts were manufactured to the same poor standard. Bill drove his P76 around town with no front bumper, front grill or body trims, and no right-hand door mirror; he was not a happy man.

Then to add to Bill's many car troubles, Leyland Australia had by then taken enough of the union's sabotaging of the Australian P76 production line. With no resolve or help coming from an unsympathetic Whitlam Labor Federal Government, Leyland Australia made a dramatic decision. They decided not only to stop the production of the P76, a car that had just been awarded by "Wheels Magazine"' the most prestigious title of "Car of the year." They also pulled out of Australia... for good.

Bill was now the not-so-proud owner of an almost new, but obsolete out-of-production Leyland P76, with many bits missing. Another sad problem became evident, he still had some four years to go on the vehicles higher-purchase payments.

At this time, the town of Kununurra and the surrounding Kimberley area were experiencing all the benefits of the massive exploration boom. The interest had now centred on finding the elusive diamond pipe, the source of all the recent alluvial diamond samples found in this area.

Other important matters were also happening in Kununurra; things that happen, and expect when a town is in the sudden, but fast expansion mode. Things like developing an eighteen-hole golf course, an absolute must-have for any modern out-back town with an average day-time temperature of thirty-eight degrees.

Then there was the formation of a water-ski club on the banks of the mighty Ord River diversion dam. When the Kununurra Hot-rod Club was formed, Bill was in his mechanical element, as this was his kind of club and he quickly became involved as part of a racing-car support team.

Everything went well for a while. In fact the racing car Bill worked on (for free) was performing quite well taking some regular first and second places, and that was the very problem. The driver was becoming famous, well... for the small town of Kununurra that is.

Morrie the hot-rod car owner and driver was only some two races away from winning the season finals. It was just about this time that Morrie accepted some additional mechanical help from an experienced race-car mechanic, a bloke suggested by a good friend in Darwin.

On this particular Saturday Bill had turned up at the racetrack at around midday to get his friend Morrie's car ready for the afternoons racing, and was staggered to find another mechanic working on his beloved hot-rod car. Bill politely enquired.

'Who the fucking hell are you, piss-off, this is my car you're working on shithead.'

Just then Morrie turned-up at the pits area to witness this unfortunate first meeting. All caused by his lack of care or consideration for all Bill's support in maintaining his hot-rod. The two mechanics were about to exchange blows, this being possibly the only matter that would drive Bill to the point of violence, and a hefty exchange of fisty-cuffs.

One must understand this was after all a very serious breach of mechanical etiquette. Morrie attempted to play-down this now explosive situation.

'Hi Bill, I see you have met Spanner. He's just arrived from Darwin, and works on the speedway cars up there. I thought you blokes might want to work together on my car, you might learn some Darwin speedway car tricks?'

Bill's response to Morrie was swift; and in a well composed meaningful Australian sentence.

'You can bloody-well get fucked Morrie, you've just blown your chances of winning the bloody hot-rod finals tonight.'

Then he marched off in the huff, jumping into his new, obsolete, out-of-production, Leyland P76 car. Spinning the wheels on the loose gravel, covering Morrie and Spanner in huge amounts of choking gravel dust.

This thoughtless action by Morrie had spun Bill into a deep pit of depression; Bill then decided to have another attempt at getting drunk... again. After some nine hours at the pub Bill was becoming more and more agitated by all the local drunks having a good time.

Much as he tried to join in, which included consuming meaningful amounts of alcohol, he could not snap out of his shitty depression. He was still in a bad and miserable mood when he overheard two blokes leaning on the bar discussing a party that was going to happen up at the Lake Argyle Tavern. Bill considered a 70 kilometre fast car trip up there was by far a better way to unwind, and possibly; well you never know, a possible chance to meet a desperate female.

Nobody in the bar wanted to join Bill for the drive up to the Lake Argyle Tavern, possibly a wise decision considering his past motoring mishaps. Then in truth, everybody knew about Bill's car crash history, Bill had quickly become a selected target within the current range of bar room jokes. In a rage of rejection, he stormed out of the pub; grabbing a bottle of rum and a cartoon of coke-a-cola from the bottle shop on his way out to the Leyland P76 in the car park. The drive up to the Lake Argyle Tavern was as they say... uneventful.

On arrival at the Lake Bill noticed the Tavern car park was full. No, it was actually overflowing with vehicles parked everywhere. He then made a direct line for the main bar, and was surprised to find the place almost deserted; except for the usual three old drunks that tended the Tavern grounds, sitting at the end of the bar.

One was tired, and rubbing his eyes. Another was leaning on the bar with his hands clapped to the side of his face, listening to the third old bloke. His hand was over his mouth having just passed a loud beer burp. Bill took in this scene with one angry glance and thought. "The three wise monkeys" see no evil, hear no evil, and speak no evil.

His boisterous arrival in the empty bar did not cause anyone to turn around or show any interest in him. Thinking they were all a bit deaf Bill made a simple but loud Australian bar request for information.

'Where the fuck has everybody gone?' Bill enquired of the three slow and none responsive drunks.

This caused a minor social reaction as trio stopped talking, smoking, and drinking. Bill could see by the looks on their faces that his interruption was not at all welcome. With a long drag on his cigarette and a wheezing sigh that drove the smoke out of his nose like a steam-train. The nearest old drunk began to explain the situation in detail to young Bill.

'Thank Christ the noisy bloody shits are all down at the boat-ramp mate, swimming with the crocs. Steve the manager o this tavern could see it was all going to end up in a big punch-up, so Steve set-up a bar down there. They were all pissed before they left here over three hours ago.'

The other drunk chipped in with his keen bit of knowledge.

'I reckons' that a few of them might git drowned or eaten by crocs a'fore the nights done mate.'

Then the third drunk just had to say something, this time it was useful information.

'If you're going to join the party down there you'll have to walk down mate, cause the access road and ramp's blocked with vehicles. Nobody can git in or out, it's a bloody mess, I hate to think what it's going to be like later when they all want to go home.'

This was exciting news for Bill, it could be a good night after all, and then a thought occurred to him.

'You blokes got any idea what the party is for, or all about?'

The last drunk spoke again. Bill was to find out later that he was by far the most sober of the three.

'It's all about some bloody car race they had today in Kununurra mate, some bloke won a race and his mechanic turned twenty-five today so they all decided to have one big bleeding celebration.'

Bill thought about this gem of information for a moment then asked.

'Don't by chance remember the winning driver's name?'

All three drunks looked up at the ceiling of the Tavern, as if seeking some sort of divine inspiration to answer Bill's simple question when a voice from behind the bar provided the answer. Olga the very large 50's something bar-maid said in her smoke-wrecked gravel voice.

'Morrie, yeah Morrie somebody, he was the winner of the car race luv, him and his mate called... Spanner I think?'

This dreadful news hit Bill like a freight-train. Now we all know that Bill has had some personal experience in this matter, having been previously hit by a freight-train. For Bill, this was indeed a powerful and sobering shock. The look on Bill's face must have triggered a deep thought of concern, as all four in the bar asked if he was all right. For big Olga the matter was clear, responding to her maternal instincts with the look of a worried fretting mother.

'What's the matter dearie; it can't be all that bad now luv. Go on and have a nice drink luv, it'll make you feel better.'

Bill was close to tears at this soothing motherly concern, if only they knew his heavy worrying problems.

Therefore, it was on that strange night, at that lonely bar in wounded remorse Bill spilt out his long sad story to four complete strangers in this remote, empty Kimberley tavern. Bill had made the bad mistake of starting at the beginning of his recent troubles, this making the story quite a bit longwinded.

Well beyond two of the drunk's bedtime as they were sound asleep at the bar long before Bill had finished his sad saga. This left Olga and old Bert to hear the end.

Olga had joined Bill in drinking double rum and cokes, managing to empty a full bottle between them. Bert on the other hand was a strict beer alcoholic, well-practiced in this drinking task, by pacing himself with skilful precision. Then placing his large beer gently on the bar and magically shuffling another cigarette from a crumpled pack, Bert spoke first...

'Well yer certainly know how ta wreck fucking cars mate, just as well I lost me drivers licence for drunk driving ten years ago, I don't have a car for you to wreck. You-know something mate... I reckon you're a bloody Medusa, a living bleeding disaster, and a pure and simple bad luck bloke to be around. And another thing I've figured... I think you're a bloody creepy bloke mate.'

Almost in tears, Bill looked sadly at Bert thinking this drunk was not offering any comfort at all in his time of need; the other sobering thought was, this drunkard might actually be right.

Bill knew all about the Medusa's touch, and had considered that he might actually have the curse. However, what was more surprising was that an old drunk in a remote area pub at the end of the world could see the resemblance to the Greek Gorgoneion and his continual bad luck. Was it just the booze talking? Then again, they do say that you always get the truth from a drunk.

Bill was now even more depressed and worried than ever, but little did he know his worries were just about to get far worse. Then again, it could be that somebody was actually listening to him, and that person was now taking a deep interest in this young Bill Gump. Who knows, if he could only understand the ways desperate females, he may yet achieve his intended mission for the drive up to the Lake Tavern?

Olga had quietly listened to Bills long sad story, and had worked out just what this young man needed most to fix all his problems... and might I add some of hers. Flashing her nicotine stained smile Olga placed her more than ample breasts on the bar, right in front of Bill's damp eyes and crooned...

'What yah say, how's about you and me going out the back for a quiet smoke, eh luv?'

Bill looked around the bar, noticed that old Bert and he were already smoking, and that Olga had made her suggestion with a fag hanging off her lower lip.

Then he looked expectantly at Bert with a dumb, glazed look on his face. The response was not what he expected.

'Fir Christ's sake mate, what's wrong with yer, she wants you to fuck her out back. You young blokes couldn't recognise a fuck if it were a Bull up a Cow.'

Bert was lonely in the sea of silence that followed that last comment. The looks on both Bill and Olga faces could kill a dead fish. Bert hunched his shoulders in defence of his observation; arms outstretched with palms upturned, displaying the typical Italian "no understand me" gesture.

'Well, what did I say wrong? It's the bloody truth, right ain't it?'

Olgas face had turned to a dark thunderous look. A frightening vision briefly flashed before Bill's eyes. If she were the Medusa, then poor old Bert would have without doubt turn to stone. With her eyes narrowing Olga rasped back at the now cringing, and bewildered Bert.

'He's just told you shithead, all about his bloody car accident and hitting that Bull up the arse while it was fucking a cow; course he knows the bleeding difference. Give the young bloke a bloody break mate, can't you see the boy's all upset at his mate winning that race this afternoon… without him.'

Olga then turned her attention back to Bill with a coy comely smile that was now a total waste of effort… Bill had gone. He had taken this lucky diversion, and opportunity to quickly vacate the Tavern bar for the car park, and his waiting Leyland P76.

It was now around ten o'clock on this dark tropical night, with only a hint of a moon. Bill remained in his parked car, listening to the chirping crickets and the croaking frogs, while finishing off the last of his bottle of rum. He was taking swigs direct from the bottle now as he had run out of coke-a-cola a while ago.

Thoughts were going through his mind, dismal thoughts, and dark thoughts. Bill was having inner doubts about his future of ever really being happy again. Nobody appeared to be interested in him, or considered his feelings no matter how hard he tried to fit in. Bill then decided on a final plan to resolve his problems... for ever.

Now suicide is a grim topic, and suicide is a word I must admit I had never heard Bill ever utter. Just as well, since the people who live in the remote North of Australia don't really care a mosquito's arse about such things. Nor do they care about the weak people who carry out such a selfish deeds... as Bill was about to find out.

The plan was quite simple. Finish off the bottle of rum, leave the seat-belt off, then set-off on the road back to Kununurra. When you get to the first long straight in the road, put your foot down hard on the go peddle and hold the steering wheel straight, dead ahead. (Please excuse the "dead ahead" pun) All very simple one would think, and might I add normally guaranteed to be most effective.

The aspen-green V8 Leyland P76 Targa Florio skidded out of the Tavern car park, Bill expertly side-slipped the tail onto the sealed road back to Kununurra. With his headlights on full high beam the car thundered down the deserted road, startling the wide-eyed Kangaroos standing begging at the side of the road, waiting as they must, to hop into the path of this bright Godly light.

Bill was travelling much too fast for their slow brains to react in time, and was long past when they had eventually decided to hop out to meet their Kangaroo light God. Then in surprise, to be left staring at the rapidly departing red tail-lights in a Kangaroo world of sad disappointment.

The Leyland picked-up speed rapidly as the first bend came into view; however, Bill knew that this first part was only a short straight. By far the best and longest straight was alongside the mountain range just after the Mistake Creek Bridge, this being about halfway to the Kununurra road junction.

Bill drove like a possessed maniac down the hill and across the Mistake Creek Bridge. At this point the road then went into a two-lane's, continuing straight for about three kilometres. Bill gripped the steering wheel hard, both hands showing white knuckles as an evil grin spread across his face, lit-up by the green glow of the dash-board lights. He then tramped the accelerator pedal hard to the floor. The big Leyland picked up speed with the dial clearly displaying an advancing 185 kilometres per hour.

As the car rapidly approached the end of the straight flat road, Bill still clearly remembers the engine noise climbing to a deafening, rattling, crescendo, as the car became airborne. A screaming noise that no self-respecting motor mechanic would ever cause or force from any motor car engine. The car vaulted the deep roadside storm-water drain, and also two old burnt-out car wrecks from some previous drunk drivers, failing to negotiate this same bend at normal speed.

Sailing through the air, Bill felt quite composed and surprised at the tranquillity of the whole event. That was until the car landed with an almighty jolt, some twenty metres out from the road bend, and down a steep slope. Everything came to an abrupt halt when the front of the car hit a solid metre high ant-hill, built around a burnt-out stout tree stump.

This sudden stop catapulted poor Bill through his newly installed windscreen with such force that he flew through the air like a cannonball. Narrowly missing two mature Ironbark trees, and then landing on his arse a further twelve metres down a steep gravel slope, finally rolling into a dry creek bed... He was only just aware that he was still holding onto the rim of his newly installed Leyland P76 steering wheel.

Bill was vigorously shaken, and most certainly stirred, although; most definitely still very much alive. This time he suffered only from a large bump to the centre of his forehead, no doubt caused when exiting the car via the windscreen. The only other painful areas were gravel rashes, caused by skidding along the ground on his arse, down the steep creek-bed.

Bill lay there for a while in the dry creek-bed deciding if this was Heaven or Hell.

It was so still and quiet, so it could be Heaven, but it was also dark as a dogs guts, so it could be Hell. Just then a flickering light caught his eye, yes he remembered he must walk into the light, that's what they do it in the movies. Bill stood up in great pain and bravely stumbled towards the flickering light. Then he heard the low but distinct noise of a car engine getting louder as the flickering light grew brighter.

'It's the Lake Argyle bloody road' he whispered aloud. 'I'm not dead after all.'

Then he felt the throbbing pain in his head and arse, and the wet feel of blood from his many bumps and scratches. Yes he was still alive but he had no idea where he was as it was still very dark so he decided to climb up the slope in the dark towards the lights.

Yes there were now other cars coming down the road from Lake Argyle. Stumbling on to the road Bill tried to wave down a car. It was only then that he realised that he was still holding on to the rim of his P76 steering wheel.

Vehicle after vehicle drove right past him, nobody would stop, many yelled out abuse to him and Bill gave them the finger. Feeling sore and tired Bill wearily sat down on a road distance marker watching yet another car approaching.

He was floodlit in the headlights and was about to throw the steering wheel away when he stopped and thought, it was after all some proof that he had just survived a terrible car accident. For want of a better place, Bill placed the wheel rim around his neck to rest his tiring arms, bowing his head in the glaring headlights of the oncoming vehicle.

To his surprise the car slowed down and stopped. Bill slowly lifted his sore head and was greeted by a bright flash, he was blinded for a moment but recognised the voice... it was Spanner, this bloke was taking a Polaroid camera picture of him.

'Hi Bill you look like shit mate,' handing him a cold beer, 'what the fuck happened to you?'

Bill was overcome by this sudden act of kindness, and was about to tell his tragic story. He then decided not-to, well not on the side of the road, suggesting that he would tell Spanner everything on the way back to Kununurra.

'Sorry mate but I'm turning right at the end of this road and going straight through to Darwin so I won't be much good to you. You'll have to get a lift from the next car that comes along mate.'

Bill was stunned into silence. He was at his worst time, he was rapidly sobering-up and the pain from his many wounds was now starting to seep through the alcohol induced relief. Spanner asked what happened to his car. Bill waved his hand in the general direction of the bush saying.

'Down there somewhere, I don't know since it's still so bloody dark, I was lucky I didn't kill myself.'

Then Bill abruptly stopped talking and his eyes rolled, thinking to himself what in hell was he saying, that was his very intention... to kill himself. Spanner noticed the change in Bill and asked if he was OK, not waiting for a reply he handed Bill a well-worn t-shirt, an old lantern torch and a half bottle of cheap scotch.

'Best I can do for now mate, there'll be another car along in a while, heaps of e'm still up there and on their way back, see you next time I'm in Kununurra bye.'

Spanner was off in a screeching wheel-spin leaving Bill standing in the middle-of-the-road with a torch in one hand, a half bottle of scotch in the other and a steering wheel rim around his neck. Bills luminous rallying watch was displayed a bright 2:10am.

Nobody came along in the next hour, and Bill had almost finished the cheap scotch, when he started to think about what had happened to his Leyland P76. Switching on the lantern torch produced nothing but a click. In a fit of rage, now quite common for Bill Gump, he threw the lantern as hard as he could into the bush.

Seconds later being quite pleased with the satisfying hollow thump, then suddenly amazed by the bright beam of light that appeared, now directed right at him. Bill followed the beam of light to the source, which just happened to be the boot of his badly bent Leyland P76.

Bill was focusing his eyes in the bright torchlight to inspect the damage. All of a sudden he noticed the vast numbers of large angry ants running all over the area lit by the lantern beam. It was just about then that Bill felt a sharp bite, the first of many hundreds of painful bites on his legs and elsewhere.

Without delay he started to brush off the hording masses of ferocious bull ants with Spanner's old t-shirt, while stamping around in a mad dance. He then quickly realised what had happened... he had crashed into a large solid bull ant's nest. A loud horn was sounding and Bill looked up towards the road to see a vehicle had stopped and a shadowy figure was standing by the open door.

The ants had got everywhere. These ants were not about to give-up on who was responsible for the total destruction of their well organised home. They were now in his shorts and under his shirt biting like hell, so he rapidly removed all his clothing while running up the slope towards the vehicle parked on the road

This was not a good day for Bill, or better described as not a good night. By the time Bill reached the road he was naked still madly brushing off the hostile biting ants with his clothes in his hands.

He ran past the man standing by the open car door and stood in the bright beam of the vehicles headlights, inspecting the damage done by the savage ants. Bills pain and frustration then drowned out by the loud laughing coming from the man in the shadows and also someone inside the car. Standing in the light of the car headlights, Bill went about closely inspecting his badly bitten equipment, as only any normal bloke would under such circumstances, only to be startled by a familiar voice.

'O'waa, would you just look at the size of that bleeding meat, I should have worked on you a bit

171

harder luv, I don't suppose you'd feel like 'arving a bit now do ya luv?'

This comment followed by a giggle and more laughter as Bert and Olga stepped out of the shadows into the light of the car headlights. Bert was all smiles with a fag stuck in the corner of his mouth, explaining the situation.

'Me and Olga don't sleep all that well, so we decided on an early start. We were on our way into town ta visit a few friends, and git the mail. Then we see's a bright light in the bush, and stop to see some bloke doing a mad dance in the nude by the light of a torch. Christ mate, you was cussing and swearing at the top of yer voice. Jesus, you looked bloody funny mate.'

Bill was embarrassed at his nudity, as he dusted off the last of the angry biting ants and pulled on his underpants and shorts that had a large hole in them from the skid along the gravel on his arse. Bert stopped grinning and became curious...

'What happened to you mate, you look like shit and where's your car, and why the hell ave you got that bloody steering wheel around your neck. Then he had a thought... Christ mate, this isn't another one of those bloody Medusa things is it?'

Bill did not want to go into a long explanation of his odd situation, thinking old Bert was closer to the truth than he dared to admit.

'It's a long painful story Bert, and I'm stuffed. If you can give me a lift into Kununurra I will tell you all about what happened on the way.'

The dawn was just breaking on yet another glorious tropical Kimberley day. Bill was sound asleep within two minutes, and never woke up until they pulled up in front of the Multi Agencies service workshop. It was now exactly ten to seven in the morning. As was normal for Bill, he was right on-time for the start of this busy day's work schedule.

Chapter: Twelve.

One can only try again

Fay the office girl stuck her head into my office.

'That old drunk gardener bloke and the fat barmaid from the Argyle Tavern are here to see you, shall I show them in?'

'What the hell do they want?'

'I dunno boss, they just asked specially to see you, but they're both grinning all over their faces about something.'

'Best show them in then.'

Olga came through the door first, closely followed by Bert both sported the reported silly big grins, and then Bert made an announcement.

'We're returning something that belongs with you mate. He needs a bit of fixing-up and some really urgent sorting out.'

I thought what in the hell are these two piss-pot bastards up-to. Last time I heard about these two, they were both going up to Darwin, having been sacked for drinking the Argyle Tavern profits.

'What makes you think that you have something that belongs to me?'

'Because mate, he is wearing your yellow "Multi Agencies" tee shirt and he says he works for you, and his name is Bill, another thing he's also out cold in our car mate. We want to drop him off right now and git going.' Olga added.' We got important things to do in town luv.'

My look must have conveyed the required surprise, as I had no idea what they were talking about, just then Pedro burst into the office.

'What's going on? Bill's in a car outside, he's either sound asleep or dead. Looks like he's banged up a bit; he must have had a pretty rough night.'

'Yea well Pedro, I was just having a chat with these Argyle Tavern people about that. Your timing is spot-on as they were just about to tell me what happened to poor old Bill.'

Bert and Olga looked at each other as if deciding who was going to tell the story, when Olga got in first with her worried motherly view of events.

'That Bill bloke is weirdly mixed-up luv. He told us about all his other car accident problems last night after he had heard that his mate Morrie and another bloke called Spanner had won some car race in Kununurra. He got very upset. We thought he was going to cry on us, everything seems to have gone wrong in his life...

Bert cut Olga off in midstream with his more direct point of view.

'He's fucking mad as a hatter if you ask me mate, and a bloody Medusa fir sure. I had told him that last night after he told us all about them car crashes he was in, well what you think he goes and does next? I'll tell you mate, he has another bloody car crash that's what. We picked him up on the Lake road just after the Mistake Creek straight bit o road; with the steering wheel off his car around his bleeding neck...

This time Olga took over the story again cutting Bert off.

'Yea he was stark ballock naked covered in angry bull ants, and dancing around like he was at some bleeding Aboriginal corroboree. He must have crashed his car in the bush somewhere hitting one of those bloody big ant hills. It sure looked a funny sight, he sure as hell is well-hung luv, and I've seen some.

Pedro and I were not interested in the size of Bill's appendages. However Pedro did, like me pick-up on the disturbing matter of Bill's apparent physical and mental state and a possible further bout of depression.

'Is Bill OK and what happened to him and to his car?'

Bert took back the story once again.

'It was still bloody dark mate so we never seen the car he was driving, but considering the way he was dancing around. I don't think he has any serious injuries apart from an almighty bump to the centre of his forehead, and about a million ant bites. After two bottles of rum and about half a dozen twenty ounce beers, I don't think your mate Bill felt a bloody thing last night.'

Bert may well be right about the level of anaesthesia Bill had consumed, but we were still very concerned. Mainly about Bill's mental state and was he okay. Bert answered our un-asked question...

'You've got a big problem with this bloke mate. Apart from being a right nut-case we think he's a bit loony; ya know, got a few screws loose up-top. If yer ask me and Olga we think he tried to write himself orff last night.'

I had my own suspicions about Bill's miserable state of mind but didn't want to get into any such discussions with these two. At that early time, I certainly didn't think Bill was in anyway suicidal, and so decided to shift the conversation along a bit, by simply pretending to misunderstand the point they were trying to make.

Then standing up, both Bert and Olga stared at me in silent expectation. I must quickly shut them up about this story, deciding best to deliver a lecture. I then put on my best political inspirational voice... and launched into a defence of Bill.

'Let me say this, Bill has a considerable capacity for the demon alcohol, well beyond that of the normal person. And so to the un-initiated, such as yourselves,' waving my hands in the general direction of these two well experienced piss-pots. 'I must admit that observing Bill for the first time in his standard drinking form. I can quite easily understand why you thought he was trying to, as you say, "write himself off." However, I can assure you this was most definitely not the case. This performance is all quite normal practice for Bill, err I mean the heavy drinking bit... So you can now see there is really nothing at all to worry about.'

Where was my camera? Both Bert and Olga stared at me with open mouths, in a look of total bewilderment firmly fixed on their faces. I took the opportunity of their stunned hesitation, by moving quickly from my desk, heading for the door passing them on the way. (Just like my Bank Manager does when he wants me to leave his office) saying...

'Well many thanks to you both for dropping in for a chat and bringing Bill back. I'm sure he will be okay now, and don't worry, we shall go and pick-up his car sometime later on today.'

They both followed me like sheep down to the workshop where we met Pedro heading back towards us. He was holding the rim of a Leyland steering wheel.

'Looks like Bill has gone into his caravan for a sleep, I'll go check-up on him and see if he's all right.'

The Argyle Tavern duo climbed into their car and left without saying another word. It was more than obvious now that they thought we were all a bit loony. I don't think my political style spin-speech did any help to convince them to change their view on Bill.

Since starting work full-time for Multi Agencies Bill had taken-up temporary residence in one of the empty West Coast Survey caravans parked in the workshop backyard. This suited him fine as he could roll out of bed in the morning, and go straight into work. He also performed the useful task of being a sort of security guard for the building. I wandered over to Bill's caravan just as Pedro was heading back to the office.

'How's Bill?' I asked noting the grin on Pedro's face as he strolled towards me.

'Oh don't worry about Bill; he's covered from head to toe, and everywhere else in nasty ant bites. He's also got this bloody big chunk out of his arse from being thrown out of the car and landing on his arse. You wouldn't believe it; he's now got a whopping big bump, this time in the middle of his forehead. He now looks like Neanderthal man. Bill's having a couple of hour's catch-up sleep, other than that I guess he's just fine.'

Bill was fine? I thought that was a tad understated. I was starting to worry about Bill, mostly about some of his bad luck events, which were by now starting to look very suspicious. Just what the hell was going on, and did Pedro have anything to add about these odd Bill events?

'Pedro those two piss pots from the Lake Argyle Tavern are quite sure that Bill was, well in their terms trying to "write himself off" in other words attempting to commit suicide, could that be true? Because if it is, he's in deep shit around here, nobody will care a rat's arse, as long as he doesn't hurt anybody in the process.'

Pedro shrugged his shoulders as he does when he was about to say something amusing.

'Bill's been trying to do himself in for quite a while, he talks about it all the time. Bill said that he has had a few goes but never quite managed to pull it off... as you've no doubt noticed.'

Thinking about this new information for a moment I replied to Pedro's casual don't give-a-damn statement.

'Yes, yes I can see that he has failed miserably in his suicide attempts, but don't you think he is just looking for some attention or something, or is it that he's just piss-poor at doing this suicide thing?'

'I don't really know Niv, but the bloke's down at the pub have given him plenty of good workable ideas on how to do it right. It wouldn't surprise me if it wasn't one of them that suggested this latest car idea, anyway it didn't work either. Back to the bleeding drawing board I suppose.'

That did sound a little callous coming from Pedro, but he was correct. Nobody in the North-West cares a damn about such attempts, and look on suicide as weak and pathetic. However, I do think the bastards down at the pub should stop encouraging Bill in his endeavours to top himself, and could have shown him a little more understanding. The bloke obviously has a problem... he could do with some real help from his mates. Not just how to exit this world.

'What do you think Pedro, you're his best mate.'

I then had a little thought, delivering my vague conclusion to Pedro...

'Could all this just be about Bill still being a bloody virgin, and his lack of having never having been laid?'

Pedro just nodded his head in silence.

'Well, it looks to me the only way we are ever going to stop Bill from doing himself in, is to get him a fuck with a consenting female. With luck, preferably a sober one, free of any sexual disease's and legal, that being one over the age of sixteen.'

I stopped talking to think about what I had just said. This is Kimberley area, that grand plan may well prove to be a much harder task than I had first thought, and then I finished off with another rallying speech.

'We, as Bills' friends, must form a cunning devious plan to achieve this life saving deflowering mission. I think we should call this new Bill help project... "Operation First Fuck."'

I was looking out of my office window and noticed Bill walking with a slight limp from his caravan over to the workshop. He had obviously showered and changed and was now talking quietly to Greg. As I came down to the workshop floor, at first glance Bill looked a right mess with a bump right in the middle of his forehead the size of a tennis ball and pulsing angry red.

'Christ Bill you don't look good old chap, why don't you go back to bed. That head bump looks very painful; we can manage the workshop jobs for today.'

Bill cracked a terrifying grin from his badly bruised face, politely replying...

'No thanks, I'm alright boss; I've had almost three hours sleep now. Anyway I've got to go get my car out of the bush on the Lake road, before someone strips the bloody thing for parts.'

Bill was absolutely right about that. Last week some poor bloke had a second puncture on their

Volkswagen beetle, and got a lift 20 kilometres into town to get both tires fixed. When they got back to the beetle an hour later both doors and the bonnet were missing, along with the engine, transmission and the other three wheels.

'You guys had better take the car break-down trailer with the winch, just in case your Leyland P76 can't be driven, well it hasn't got a steering wheel now, has it? Pedro can go with you to give a hand. Anyway Bill, you don't look like you should be doing any driving for a while.'

They were both gone for about two hours when the Land Cruiser with the car trailer attached pulled into the workshop yard. It was obvious Bill's P76 was a total write-off this time. The vehicle was just a mangled pile of twisted Aspin green metal. The front was totally smashed-in, driving the engine and gearbox back into the car's interior. Newtons Second Law of motion obviously saved Bill's life that night as he, being the lighter mass, most certainly left the car's front seat through the front windscreen, just before the engine occupied the same space he was sitting in. Pedro, Bill, and I were staring at the crumpled car on the trailer when the mild-mannered Pedro made an intelligent, and significant observation.

'You know something Bill; if that ant hill was just a foot higher you would have been killed by it when you went through the front screen. Also, if you had your seat belt on; the engine and gearbox would have got you for sure, when it ploughed backwards into the cabin area.

I could see where you landed, just missing two solid trees on your way through the air. Then you were lucky again by landing on your arse, and not your head, then lucky yet again to land on the gentle sloping grassed side of the creek bed. By all accounts Bill, you should be fucking dead.'

I was listening to Pedro's detailed description of Bill's car crash, and thinking... was this just another bit of Bill's good luck? I mean after all the bloke was trying to write himself off right, so it wasn't just an unfortunate bad luck accident.

Something out there, maybe some God was telling Bill he still had a future in this world. The other good thing that came out of this... err accident, was that Bill had fallen quite a bit behind in his car payments. Yes that's right, the higher purchase car payments on his now seven month old out-of-production, obsolete Leyland P76 car.

However, as luck would have it, Bill's Leyland still had the first year's comprehensive insurance cover on it for its full value. Furthermore, the insurance company did actually pay out the total higher purchase debt on the car, and also let Bill keep the wreck.

Now you would have to agree, that was also a bit of good luck. As a consequence, Bill now has no bill's, (to avoid the pun make that) no debt's, but now he has no car and no other means of transport... could this also be a good thing… who would know?

One would hope that without a vehicle Bill would have reduced his possible means, or tools, to accomplish his grim mission. This may well be so, but now we had one almighty problem to consider. We now had a confirmed admission to what was previously only just a suspicion... That is, Bill Gump has openly admitted the fact that he was actually trying to commit suicide.

Chapter: Thirteen.

A sign of our time

We were all keeping a close eye on Bill Gump, and he knew it. The little bit of extra attention seemed to quieten him down, but he soon got cranky again, mainly because he no longer had a vehicle to get around in. Pedro started to lend Bill his company supplied Holden Ute, we had two of these Holden Ute's both identical, one I used and the other was supplied as part of Pedro's job as workshop manager.

We were kind-of proud of our company Holden utilities as they were beautifully sign-written by the one and only Bluey Davidson owner of "A Sign of our Time." Bluey was very much old school in the sign-writing business, everything was done by his skilled hand, and might I say artistically done. Every job was a virtual work-of-art, there were no stick-on signs ever seen in Bluey's sign shop.

When I first met Bluey, he was on his way to nowhere from Perth with three boozy friends aptly named Macker, Noddy, and Boofer. They had stopped in Kununurra to fill up Bluey's old FJ Holden sedan at the BP garage, on their way to nowhere in particular. But planning to end-up back home in Melbourne, who knows when. Bluey was in deep trouble; his old car had refused to start again, tempers at the BP fuel pumps were heating up.

The BP staff wanted Bluey and his old Holden off the fuel pump area, and Blueys mates Macker, Noddy, and Boofer were threatening physical violence to anybody who was game enough to try moving them.

Within a short time, Blueys battery had died a graceful death swinging over the well-worn motor one last time. The next move was predictable; the four of them went about attempting to push-start the old Holden, therefore resolving the first problem of vacating the pump area… and a mighty punch-up at the BP service station.

Being an observer to this spectacle, I could see that some form of help was required. We tried using the jump-start cables from my workshop Ute, but that didn't work either.

I had never seen a car with a six-volt battery system before except in a museum. The engine whizzed over like crazy with the full twelve volt jumper cables connected, driving the old six volt starter, but it still refused to ignite into life as a running engine.

What caught Greg the mechanics attention, was that after removing the jumper cables, the engine continued to spin over for a few seconds more. Greg then provided Bluey with a very qualified and accurate diagnosis of his grim automotive problem...

'This engines fucked mate; no bloody compressions, you're going nowhere in that heap of shit today pal. If I were you mate, I'd find somewhere to camp for the night and then go down the pub and get drunk.'

This was shattering news for Bluey. (His travelling companions had already gone down to the pub.) Bluey was not what you would call a mechanically gifted person in any way, having bought the old car in Perth from someone who was described as a good friend.

This huge purchase had drained Bluey's financial resources of most of his available cash. However, the old FJ Holden did get Bluey around Perth for a while, becoming a reliable old friend for both work and play, and now while travelling... his only home.

He talked about his old car as if it were a dying friend; it was now obvious to me that Bluey had become quite attached to his old motor car. It was most likely, if not the biggest financial investment he had ever made in his life.

At that time Bluey must have been around 32 years old, but acted, and dare I say, looked much older. He was a little guy; only about five foot two in the old measurement, with a shock of bright red hair, no doubt the very reason why he was known as Bluey.

Later that day down at the pub he told me in a sad voice all about his beloved car, how he had saved-up and bought the car for cash. He was born in Melbourne, and brought up in a hard socialist background, to believe that buying things on the tick or HP was a vice and a scourge inflected by the rich capitalists on good hardworking people.

He was still confused and upset, and having a problem coming to terms with the fact that this might be the end of the road for his beloved old FJ Holden. The car had never let him down until now; it had been a big part of his life for so long. As is the way with all these talented artistic types, Bluey was a very sensitive man, and was only a choking mouthful of beer away from bursting out into a flood of crocodile tears.

I whispered into his ear that this was the north-west of Australia, and men expected to be men. Crying in the pub when perfectly sober was a big no-no around here, not like Melbourne, or some parts of Perth like Fremantle. He then quickly pulled himself together and sighed, pouting lower lip like a two-year old.

'What can I do, I don't have the money to stay in town long, and I don't have much money left to fix the engine on my car.'

Quick-as-a-flash old big ears down at the other end of the bar suggested that he should just buy a second-hand engine from the Arab. Now big ears worked exclusively for the Arab, and he did in fact have a remarkably large set of ears. The only thing was that they did in fact work quite well.

As for the Arab, well he wasn't really an Arab at all, but he did look like one, and some would say acted like one. His real name was Terry, the man who managed the town rubbish collection and the dump. He also owned the local car wreckers yard.

All said and done he was quite a nifty, or should that be shifty, businessman. The Arab always had a suspicious deal or two on the go, and was also quite a stud with the ladies... well, so I have been told. However it was now more than obvious that he was also quite colour-blind, which explained quite a few things in this very remote Kimberley town.

Much as I tried, I couldn't steer Bluey away from the tempting deal of another engine from the Arab, I was losing ground fast to a much more powerful and convincing influence. Big-ears being a known master at slight-of-hand dealings, and having a remarkable and powerful level of bullshit quickly gained Bluey's willing attention... and ultimately his money.

They do say that had big-ears gone into Australian politics, instead of working for the Arab, he would have most likely ended up as leader of the Federal Labour party. (I out-rightly refuse to spell labour without the "u." I think that when the party was first formed under the tree of knowledge in Queensland in 1891, the new political party was going through a bad spell (excuse the pun.) The bad spelling was eventually traced back to a bloke called King O'Malley, an American evangelist who registered the Labor party name in the late 1800's. Not only was O'Malley never naturalised, he could not spell, also claiming he did not know his correct date of birth, using the date 4th July 1854. This being so, it made him ineligible to sit in any Australian parliament... but he did.

To cover this gross spelling error, the Labour party concocted a typical cover-arse political spin story. As the elected Australian Minister for Home Affairs, the American born King O'Malley was hell-bent on getting a reform policy passed to use all American bad spelling in Australia. The O'Malley reform policy never passed into law; hence the Labour party was stuck with a misspelt political party name.

So now you know how the Australian Labour party first went wrong in politics, they could not even spell their own bloody name correctly. Some say they have never recovered from this gross error and have continued to make bigger, and more serious errors ever since. Then again, I did hear they may have just given their "U" to the unions... I mean to say, they are very close partners aren't they... well who the hell would know?)

The next time I saw Bluey was a few days later. He was vigilantly watching his beloved FJ Holden being roughly towed up and down the town's main street by the Arab in an effort to start the new...err second-hand engine.

I was standing alongside Bluey watching this unusual town spectacle, when all of a sudden there was an almighty loud bang. The engine had suddenly come to life with the Arab pumping and revving the engine like a madman to keep it going. The entire vehicle and half the road now engulfed in a thick blue/black smoke, which gently wafted away leaving a thick stream of black smoke streaming out of the car's exhaust pipe.

Bluey looked quite pleased at this early successful start scene, and turned to Greg my mechanic who had stopped by at the sound of the loud explosion. Bluey then made the big mistake of asking him...

'What do you think mate, will she get me home to Melbourne?'

Greg grimly stared at the billowing smoke pumping out from the exhaust, pushed his glasses back up to the bridge of his nose and replied in his normal abrupt manner.

'That engines fucked mate. I doubt it would get you out of town, let alone all the way over to Melbourne. You know something mate; I reckon your old engine was in far better nick than that one. A set of piston rings, and a few gaskets would have got the bloody thing going again.'

Bluey looked totally stunned at this vicious and very blunt observation from the mild, scholarly looking Greg, then spluttered out his response in disbelief.

'Why the hell didn't you say that you could fix my old engine, what can I do now, I've run out of bloody money?'

Still watching this strange scene taking place in the main street of Kununurra, Greg was quick to tell Bluey the blunt and honest truth... yet again.

'Far as I remember mate, you never asked us about fixing your old engine. You just went out and bought that heap of shit engine from the Arab. Want some more free advice... are you listening this time mate. Talk to my boss, he's standing right next to you, maybe we can make one good engine out of the two heaps of crap, with luck that might get you around town for a while.'

Then Greg, the man of few words, but a heart of gold turned, and walked back to the workshop. Nevertheless, we both clearly heard him say as he departed.

'Best of luck to you mate in getting your old engine back from the Arab, without paying the bastard again.'

Well the Arab actually did give bluey back his old engine, and at no cost. The reason was simple; the Arab was there when Bluey told us both what he did for a living... He was a commercial sign-writer.

Now the Arab was a smart man, who was no dill when it came to making a quick buck. He could see all too clearly the many advantages in having a commercial sign-writer in town. Both the Arab and I tried to convince Bluey he had a ready-made job in setting up a sign-writing business in Kununurra, however Bluey was a man very much set in his ways. I will never forget the look on his face, and will always remember his dismissing words in reply to our suggestion that he should stay and go into the sign business.

'I'm packing-up "the whole box and dice" and going up to Darwin, on my way home to Melbourne with me mates, "I could paint this fucking town out in a month." Why the hell would I want to stay in this arsehole of a place?'

That was the first of many times I would hear Bluey say that very Victorian Melbourne phrase, "the whole box and dice."

Apparently, Blueys huge travelling adventure started, when after many years of convincing talk by his boozy mates, they all decided to leave the daily rut of Melbourne for a while, and to try a spell of working in sunny Perth.

Consequently it was to be in that October of 1968, that Bluey and three of his boozy friends. Macker, Noddy, and Boofer set off by slow train for the mind-numbing, boring, three day train journey across the empty Nullarbor Desert. Heading for sunny City of Perth in the West, and hopefully a brave new world of experience in the West.

They all stayed at a low budget single men's hostel called The Cloisters in St George's Terrace. Eventually all found jobs, settling into the slow Perth lifestyle, and yet another dreary city. At least Melbourne had some night-life, and colourful crims.

They hung on for a miserable long two and a half long years. Then that was it, they had all had enough, Perth was no better than Melbourne, it was time to go home.

On arrival in Perth Bluey had purchased an old FJ Holden sedan, a vehicle he needed for his work. This bold decision had cost Bluey the last of his small savings, all agreed this was their insurance, an exit ticket, being a future means of escape from Perth back home to Melbourne… and now that time had arrived.

The departure plan was a simple one. They would pick-up their last pay-packets on the Friday night, and then all four would go celebrate their exodus from dull Perth, with a boozy night out down at the local pub.

It was here that things started to go a little wrong, with a late unanimous decision made, when the pub closed, they should get on the road for home. The plan was to head east to Southern Cross, Coolgardie, and Norseman to pick-up the Eyre Highway across the Nullarbor to the Eastern states and home to Melbourne. Noddy, the smart one, reckoned that as they were all going to live rough in their swags, why bother hanging around Perth until morning... they might as well get on the road now.

Now for some strange and unexplained reason, they missed the A94 road-turn to the east and continued driving north on the A95. This was the inland road through New Norcia, Meekatharra, and Newman, ending up in Port Hedland in the far North of Western Australia. This was opposed to driving east on the A94 straight across the Nullarbor desert, retracing the way they had originally came to Perth on the train.

Might I add the first plan would have been a saving of some 4100 kilometres and eight days travelling? I just had to ask Bluey the obvious question, why the hell did he decide to continue driving north all the way up through Newman, Port Hedland, and Kununurra to get to Melbourne?

He looked at me as if I had asked him some sort of crazy question, and then he replied in all honesty... 'We just followed the bloody road signs mate.'

There is no doubt that Bluey liked a beer or two, and I do suspect that his three friends liked a few more. It was at about this time that I realised that Bluey was brilliant at creating signs, but hopeless at reading them.

As with all matters of a non-urgent nature, they eventually resolve themselves in due time. Blueys boozy pals soon found a free lift on a truck bound for Katherine and Darwin and left town suddenly, leaving Bluey behind.

When Bluey discovered this, he let-out a mighty mournful curse, then sat down and drank another stubby of beer.

He then sighed in accepted defeat, opened up his well-used, paint splashed, wooden box of little pots of paint and camel hair brushes, and went to work doing what he does best... sign-writing.

The Arab was the first in town to sport his very own new roadside sign.

"Kununurra Town Rubbish Tip
Turning 2 miles or 5 kilometres on the right.
No Dumping Rubbish.
No shooting.
No Stealing things without paying.
Tip entry fee $2.00 cash along the finger.
By Order of the tip contractor."

The sign-writing on my two workshop Ute's was the envy of the town, and nothing less than magnificent. This was not just any old boring sign-writing, but beautiful works of art, being hand-drawn, with full colour dealer logos, cartoons; murals, and pictures.

I soon discovered, Bluey was not a sign-writer at all... he was an accomplished artist. This little man had a special talent, a talent that even the cunning Arab could see, and make good use of. Soon Bluey had more sign-writing work than he could handle for a long, long, time.

I must admit that I did have my suspicions that the Arab had a lot to do with Bluey's pal's getting that convenient truck lift out of town.

In closing, Bluey was right; he did paint the town out; however, it was many times over in his long stay in Kununurra of over forty years. Bluey still remains as a long-time, permanent resident, and town character of Kununurra. At the young age of seventy-four, he is still painting the town out to this very day...

I wish you a long healthy life Bluey. You have filled this world of yours and others with colour and good advice. What more can a man want as a legacy in this life. I am proud to have known you.

Chapter: Fourteen.

Believe me I wasn't even trying

Pedro had just recently got back from a business trip to Darwin, and while there had bought a very cheap second-hand Leyland P76 V8 from Deso at Port Darwin Motors. These vehicles were now selling second-hand at ridiculously low prices at around $300 to $400.

The Whitlam Labour government had done an excellent job on destroying the manufacturer's reputation of this all-Australian designed and built vehicle. Nobody wanted one, well... except Pedro. Pedro was still very much in love with his new toy, when Bill Gump came up and asked if he could borrow the car for the weekend, to go out to the local speedway-track.

Pedro cringed at this request, having remembered what Bill had done to his last Leyland P76. As such, decided that Bill could borrow his workshop Holden

Ute instead. I guess you should make that "my" Holden Ute.

Bill was not a man to hold any grudges, and had long since made-up with Morrie over the unspeakable matter of the Darwin mechanic working on his hot-rod. Bill was now back, happy as ever, working on the hot-rod car every weekend. Morrie had now moved out to stay at a place called Packsaddle Plains, being some twenty kilometres away, as he was now employed by a company called Dessert Seeds.

This new job was quite a good deal for Morrie, as the speedway track was only some five kilometres further down the road, and Morrie now had the full use of the Dessert Seeds service workshops. The only disadvantage for Bill was Dessert Seeds was a fifteen-minute drive out of town. This distance was no longer a problem now as Bill had the use of a vehicle, the beautiful, just completed sign-written workshop Holden Ute.

It was a very pleasant, sunny Saturday morning, when Bill drove out to see Morrie at Packsaddle to get some work done on the stock car. He was in deep thought about tonight's all important race meeting, staring blankly out of the windscreen, as you do when in deep thought.

He had become very aware of a fast approaching bull-bar, firmly fitted to the Toyota Landcruiser heading towards him into town. The Toyota driven by Ross Birken. He was in a mess, franticly rushing into the town pub to stabilise his alcoholic withdrawal, and physical trembling condition, gained from last night's boozy Friday night party at Dessert Seeds.

Ross, with his eye's half closed in squinting pain, was suffering from a king-size hangover... and the dreaded shakes. Thinking a cigarette might help a little, he was attempting to light one. However it was presenting an unsynchronised problem, on this bright sunny morning.

Then as luck would have it, Ross managed to suck just at the right time as the shaky lighter flame passed the end of his wobbling fag... he was alight. He was going to make it to the pub, with at least one of his vices in fully satisfied, and in operational condition. Then catastrophe struck, he dropped the bloody thing between his legs.

As was the norm for most working males in the north-west, Ross was wearing his very short, well-worn, and thin footy shorts. He suddenly experienced the hot uncomfortable sensation that his balls were on fire...and they were.

Ross immediately plunged his hand between his legs to retrieve the lost burning fag. While Ross was head-down identifying the extent of the damage to his family jewels, he suddenly experienced, no felt, a loud shuddering bang and spun off the road into a stout tree. Apparently the only tree this side of the road for many kilometres.

Bill was amazed at the oncoming vehicles' antics, it was suddenly all over the road. No matter which way he steered, the approaching vehicle steered into his path. Then came a tearing bang as he slammed on the brakes. Bill said to himself, no screamed aloud to the heavens.

'Oh fuck I've gone and done it again, what will the boss think this time?'

The Ute came to a screeching halt in the middle-of-the-road and Bill got out examining the extent of the damage. He first noticed surprisingly, that the driver's door opened quite well. Bill was thinking this was a good sign indeed, and then he looked at the side of the Ute.

The complete side of the Ute was smashed in with the metal ripped open in various places from the front headlight to the rear tail-light. Then Bill looked up and around to see who had caused this. There were no other vehicles on the road as far as he could see in either direction except the Toyota that had sideswiped him now parked against a lone tree, some thirty metres down the road.

Ross came slowly walking back down the road towards Bill, shaking his sore head...

'Sorry about that mate, I dropped me bleeding fag in me bleeding lap and it was burning my balls, I think I have third-degree burns down there now.'

Bill was not amused or interested, his temper rising by the second.

'You fucking idiot, we were both almost killed in a head-on crash over your stupid bloody cigarette.'

'Now calm down Bill,' Ross breaking into a wide amusing grin. 'I'm sure that your boss has insurance to cover all this bloody damage; my Toyota only has a bent bull-bar, so that won't cost him much to fix mate.'

That don't-care-a-damn comment just made Bill cringe with spluttering rage. Then raising his voice, and his fists, Bill screamed…

'You fucking shithead, you caused this bleeding crash not me, your insurance is going to pay for all this damage.'

Ross cut into Bill's rage as they both stood threateningly facing each other off, eyeball to eyeball, Ross declaring aggressively in a slow determined voice.

'I don't have any insurance mate so I hope your boss has, it's his bloody Ute isn't it?'

Bill reached out, about to grab Ross' shirt and stopped. Ross stood his ground and stared his steely hard blue eyes into Bill's eyes, and then Bill started to remember a few things. Ross was an accomplished bar-room brawler of some considerable note, and was with his well-practised and honed skill, always on the winning side in any pub fight.

This could get ugly, very ugly indeed. For a man in alcoholic withdrawal with a severe bout of the shakes, Ross was putting on a very convincing show. Bill wisely backed off from this threatening position then in a defeated voice.

'I reckon that you've just got me the bloody sack. Hells fire and shit man; we just got this bloody Ute sign-written. It was only finished yesterday. You've not only fucked up the company workshop Ute, but my job too. Thanks a lot pal as that's all I need in the world right now.'

Ross took a step back and dropped his clenched fists as the threat of a fight was now gone, then noticing Bill's obvious distress he then tried some "matey talk" in an attempt to console Bill, and lighten up the mood.

'For Christ's sake Bill, stop your worrying mate; I'll go tell your boss it was all my fault. He can't sack you if it wasn't your bloody fault can he. He'd be a piss-weak bastard if he did. I'll go see him right now,' then thinking... 'well maybe in about an hour's time after I've had a few beers at the pub.'

Bill thought about this strategy for a few seconds, then suggested.

'Is that a good idea, I mean you going down to the pub first, and then going to see my boss. I don't think my boss would take it too well, being told about this bloody Ute crash from a pissed-up bloke... especially by the very bloke who caused it?'

Ross ignored Bill's comment and slipped into a mood of assurance.

'There you go again mate, all over worrying about nothing. I know your boss; anyway he'll most likely be down at the pub when I get there. I can sort of well, just let it slip out in normal conversation, and then tell him about this unfortunate bit o trouble. You'll see, it'll be all right mate... trust me.'

Bill did not look convinced at this attempted assurance, but then again, in the circumstances what could he do. After all, it was most likely better that the boss should hear the bad news first, from the one who had caused the smash. Bill was definitely right on that score; however, for another very good reason. The point may not have crossed Bill's confused mind, but I was quite relieved to hear that this was a genuine accident and not another... well who knows.

Consequently, it was later on that same day at around two o'clock, then deciding to have a quick drink at the pub on my way home from work. I had just taken delivery of my ordered beer when a loud bellowing voice blasted out from the worker's bar. The booming voice, cutting across the open beer garden bar and into the cave bar, where I was sitting quietly, about to enjoy my first drink of the day.

'Dallas you old bugger, I just sideswiped your fancy bloody Holden Ute this morning while coming into the pub. It's kinda fucked-up all down one side; sorry mate, it was my fault. It was an accident mate. I dropped me fag between me legs and burnt my balls. Oh yeah Bill looks pretty pissed, I mean to say not drunk pissed, but well sort of unhappy. You might want to check-up on him… you know.'

Ross then held his head to one side, with his tongue hanging out in a classic dead hangman's look. It was obvious to all in the bar that Ross was being more than a little insensitive, regarding Bill's known pent on self-destruction. The whole pub burst out into ruckus piss-pot laughter. I was not about to defend Bill in a twenty metre shouting conversation through two bars, especially with one of the local town drunks. I decided I had heard all I needed to hear on the subject, finished my drink and went home.

Bill came around to my house on the Sunday morning, he was full of genuine apologies telling me all about his bad luck, and near head-on collision with a Toyota Landcruiser. He was upset and miserable, much more than normal, as he was sure I would fire him on the spot.

Well if he had come around yesterday, right after the accident, in mad frustration I most likely would have. Now I had simmered down, realising that this accident was unlike all of Bill's other car accidents. It was after all just another example of Bill's bad luck, then again was it good luck, as the chances were of this accident being a full head-on collision. One in which Bill would have surely not have survived, and this was not even an attempted, well... er suicide.

A thought flashed across my mind; maybe Bill really was a Martian… Could he have been saved time and again by some great spiritual power? No, I must dismiss those thoughts, who in hell up here in the Kimberley would want to save Bill, and for what reason.

We do after all live in a cruel world of mostly selfish, self-centred people. A world that nice guys like Bill have problems big with.

Was that a contradiction? Possibly, but then again, none of Bill's actions and problems make sense to bloke's like me or Pedro; or ninety nine percent of all the other people, who have chosen to live in this remote north-west of Australia.

Then again, when we make a promise in the north, we keep it. We were all still very much committed to helping Bill achieve total success with Operation First Fuck.

Over the coming months we had set-up a few female introductions but nothing eventuated. Bill was being too nice a gentleman to notice the normal come-on female signals, and was not aggressive enough in the stakes to out-manoeuvre the fierce male opposition, thereby losing his chance of finding a soul mate. Pedro reckoned we had a major, or maybe an impossible task on our hands.

On a number of occasions we had to back off our mission efforts, as the ladies in question thought we were the interested party. This helping-a-mate thing was starting to have serious future matrimonial ramifications. Continuing with such a zealous, and unabated mission could have obvious and bad consequences, as both Pedro and I were married... and this was after all a very small town.

Chapter: Fifteen.

Sorry I have lost your Toyota

Pedro had a plan. Not a great plan, but a plan nonetheless, and that was to keep Bill flat-out. So busy, that he would not have any time to think of anything but work. We all agreed, this would be a good interim idea, but we should still keep a look-out for any depressive symptoms. We must try to get Bill involved as much as possible in everything we did.

This strategy worked for a while, but as the weeks whizzed past, we could see we were gradually losing the game. Sending Bill off on as many trips into the bush repairing and servicing vehicles was always a less stressful time for me. Bill was a man that prided himself on getting the job done, and he'd have to be alive to do that, so we just knew he would always come back.

I was just thinking we've run out of bush jobs for Bill, when Fay the office girl breezed into the office and dumped a hire file on my desk.

'I think you should take a look into this hire boss. We were supposed to get an RFDS (Royal Flying Doctor Service) call from Kalumburu that is if this guy ever got there.'

Glancing at the file I noticed this was the Wentworth hire; one of my Toyota Landcruisers, unit number four. I remembered that it was me who reluctantly hired this vehicle out some six weeks ago to Senator Bill Wentworth, ex Federal Liberal Minister for Aboriginal affairs, and his wife Barbara. The plan was for them to visit Kalumburu Mission, and a number of other indigenous settlements in the Mitchell Plateau area on a farewell visit after his recent retirement from politics.

These are very remote parts of the Kimberley, and required a traveller to have a certain level of bush survival skills and knowledge. The Senator had spent a lifetime in politics convincing people that he knew what he was talking about, and had managed to convince me that he was more than qualified to handle the Toyota 4X4 in a remote area. Adding he had previously driven to Kalumburu and other remote indigenous areas a number of times before without incident.

Signing up this vehicle hire was to be my first, and only, face to face meeting I would ever have with the quietly spoken, Honourable William Charles Wentworth AO…

Bill, the name he prefers, was somewhat indignantly set back at my prodding questions as to what sort of equipment he intended to carry with him. He scoffed in denial, when asked if I could have a quick look at the map he intended to use. At that meeting I had detected a strong whiff of aloof, self-centred know-all arrogance. The very manner of attitude that can easily get a man killed in the remote Australian out-back.

I looked down at the Senators driving licence, confirming he was seventy-one years old. Then at the frail man sitting in front of me, and then to his lovely smiling, totally trusting wife. I was in the middle of drawing breath to refuse to hire the vehicle, when Barbara Wentworth interjected in a clear steady voice.

'You won't need to worry about us young man; we have been to many remote Aboriginal camps over the years. We will be all right you'll see.'

I now wish I had stayed with my first instincts about this particular hire, as the final outcome was not what anyone would have expected... or wanted.

With the decision made, I then hired a fully equipped Toyota Landcruiser to Senator Bill on our standard Multi Agencies hire form, having a return date in six weeks. According to the agreed return date, the vehicle was now three days overdue.

Noted on the hire form was that Senator Bill had agreed to make an RFDS radio call, confirming that he had arrived safely at Kalumburu Mission. This is what Fay had picked-up on, now he was not only overdue, but we had not received any RFDS safety call.

I made a quick phone call to Peter the RFDS radio operator in Derby. Peter confirmed that Senator Bill Wentworth and his wife had been, and left Kalumburu Mission over a week ago, also that he had no instructions to pass on any information to me.

Next was a call to the Hotel Kununurra, the answer nearly made me fall off my chair, I was advised that Senator Wentworth, and his wife had checked out of the Hotel Kununurra last Wednesday, four days ago.

Another phone call to Ansett our local airline, confirmed that the Senator and his wife had departed for Darwin last Wednesday on the midday flight. Apparently all happy and smiles about their very memorable out-back road trip to Kalumburu Mission. Just how memorable this trip was I was soon to find to find out.

The plot and story was becoming very strange indeed, and what the hell had happened to my almost new, only eight months old fully equipped Toyota Landcruiser?

After three frustrating days of trying to reach Senator Bill by phone, I was having my suspicions that the senator was doing a good job of avoiding me. A new and cunning strategy was required. I left a message with one of the Senators people that an important matter regarding Kalumburu needed discussing and to call this number urgently. That did the trick, and I was lucky that I answered the call. A soft controlled voice returned my call.

'Bill Wentworth here, someone wishes to talk with me regarding a matter at Kalumburu.'

'Ah yes Senator that would be me, my names Niven Dallas and the matter is about your recent trip to Kalumburu.' I could sense that Bill had no idea who I was. 'The matter I wish to discuss with you sir, is what happened to my almost new Toyota Landcruiser that you hired from my company some two months ago?'

Bill let slip a small gasp being surprised at my direct question; however, he quickly recovered his complete composure replying in a gentle voice.

'I have sent you a letter regarding that matter; you should have received it by now, the letter explains everything.'

'Well unfortunately I have not received any letter, but I would assume correctly that you have hired a vehicle before. The normal practice is to return the vehicle at the agreed date and time to the depot that you hired it from, Senator this vehicle is now well and truly overdue, and technically missing, now presumed stolen. Why in hell would you just jump on a plane to Darwin without contacting me, the owner of the vehicle to explain what's happened?'

There was a nervous rustling as the phone moved about, then the gentle voice recovered and continued.

'The vehicle broke-down, and my wife and I had to walk for over five hours in thick bush until we came out on to the Great Northern Highway north-east of Halls Creek. We were very lucky, as a road train came along just as we found the road. We managed to wave it down and got a lift into Kununurra. The truck got in at about eleven, so we had just enough time to have a shower and catch the midday jet to Darwin.'

I thought to myself this guy must be having me on... he must be having some sort of expensive joke with me. From Kalumburu Mission back to the Gibb River Road, is around about two hundred and sixty kilometres of very rough gravel road.

This silly old fart is telling me, that on the way back from Kalumburu Mission, he somehow missed the Gibb Road, then failed to turn in the direction of Kununurra. He had then continued on, by crossing the Gibb River Road into the wild remote bush, then kept going south through the dessert bush towards Halls Creek, which is some two hundred kilometres away. By all accounts the Senator and his wife should be dead.

'Senator, this story is almost unbelievable, nonetheless that was over a two weeks ago, where the hell's my Toyota Landcruiser right now?'

There was a small hesitation then came the came a rather smug reply.

'Quite frankly, I can't tell you where your vehicle is right now, as I just don't know. I am sorry I have lost your Toyota. All I can say is it's somewhere in the bush about five hours walking distance from the Great Northern Highway on the Kununurra side about ninety kilometres from Halls Creek.'

'For fucks sake Senator Wentworth, you have just given me a possible vehicle position within two hundred square kilometres, in a remote dessert. The only thing I have to work on is the vehicle is positioned, somewhere between the Gibb River road and the Great Northern Highway. That's over one hundred and eighty kilometres between the two roads; anyway what the hell were you doing south of the Gibb River road?'

The pause to reply, was I sensed, one of minor embarrassment. The voice then quickly regained strength, with a burst of resolute, political style, smug confidence.

'Well if you must know on my way back from Kalumburu Mission I missed the turn on to the Gibb River Road, obviously accidentally crossing the road and got a little lost. I reasoned that if I continued to drive due south I would eventually come out onto the Great Northern Highway at some point, unfortunately your unreliable vehicle broke down.'

'Unreliable, how's that Bill, the bloody thing was only eight months old, what went wrong to cause the break-down?'

'As far as I could observe the radiator had developed a leak and lost all the water. Then the engine overheated and stopped, it then refused to turn over as I believe the battery was also flat.'

I could tell by the phone attitude that I was starting to piss the Senator off, he didn't like my questions, and my prodding remarks on his obvious stupidity, or my view of... anything. I on the other hand was rapidly forming the opinion, that the Senator was a complete and utter bush idiot. A man who had a total disregard for safety and common sense, and much preferring to rely on lady luck?

The Senator had broken all the standard and acceptable rules when travelling in a remote area. The rules are very simple, and will keep you alive. Tell someone of your travel plans and intentions. Never leave your vehicle if it breaks down. If you must move away from your vehicle leave information of your intention, date, time, direction and provisions carried, and lastly and most importantly mark the vehicle location well. These simple rules were on labels plainly visible, stuck on all my four wheel drive Toyota sun visors.

The Senator may have been in a very remote area; however, the light aircraft traffic in that area is quite regular. Bill could have easily signalled a passing aircraft using a vehicle mirror. Following which he would have been rescued and back in Halls Creek or Kununurra within hours of being found, and then I would have known where my Toyota Landcruiser was.

I don't think Senator Bill realised the level of danger he had exposed himself, and his lovely lady too. Trekking through the rough bush for five hours in the tropical heat would have been a tough call for a fit thirty year old, and nearly impossible when you're in your seventies. This proves that Bill and Barbara were indeed very fit and tough old people.

However, we will never really know what level of stress Bill and Barbara went through, during that gruelling five hours of being lost. Totally lost in one of the most remote and uncomfortably hot places in Australia. Did he know how lucky he was to stumble out onto a bitumen road, the Great Northern Highway, eighty kilometres east of Halls Creek… then with some further luck as a Mack road train was passing?

I will give some credit to Bill that his theory of heading south, eventually hoping to come across the Great Northern Highway was sound, but his reasoning to do this, as a choice, was all wrong, very wrong.

I for one have never had, or tempted such a level of luck, and I doubt if many others can claim such a run of good luck. Then again, it is said that good luck is mostly created through positive thinking by denying all negative thinking.

However, we have all seen that bloody-minded ignorance and pride can provide the same sort of assurance. What you don't know about anything can't hurt you, right. I would be hard pushed to put my life or my loved ones future on such a theory.

This only leaves the macho male matter of pride; now in his advancing years, this would be called saving face. Good one old boy, tally-oh old chap for King and country and all that crap.

While all this was going through my mind I became aware of a polite cough on the other end of the phone, realising that I must have stopped talking.

'Senator Bill, I must inform you that my intention is to send you an account for the replacement cost of the lost vehicle, and the hire account to date, and I will expect this account to be paid promptly.'

Senator Bill was apparently not moved by my statement, and remained silent in a show of zero emotion. I again sensed that he did not take kindly to my blunt demand, and then replied in his gentle controlled voice.

'Your vehicle breaking down was the cause of all this drama. Your unreliable vehicle could have possibly been the reason and basis of a tragedy. I will forward any correspondence from you to my legal people after which you will then be required to deal direct with them on this matter.'

There came a sharp click as the Senator hung-up the phone, indicating that our conversation had terminated. I glared at the silent phone, as if daring the thing to come back to life again, and it did. Fay stuck her head into my office and advised me there was someone on the other line trying to get through but I would have to hang the bloody phone up first which I did. It was Lindsay Doig the local operations manager of Stockdale Prospecting.

'Hi Niven, lost any of your fine vehicles lately, and possibly a client or two whose bones are now lying bleaching in the hot sun in some lonely dessert?

Lindsay was always the dramatic humourist. I guess being a Scotsman gave him some sort of expected right to this type of cynical humour. Then again being a Scotsman myself I had a full appreciation of his style and charm, as such we got along quite well.

Lindsay was a good looking, tall six foot four Geologist, with an easy smile and a quick wit. Unfortunately his success and ability to make people laugh, in no way matched any success in his ability to find diamonds. There was always a percentage of truth in Lindsay's cynical humour and he did have my full attention.

'What's this all about Lindsay, spent too much time looking for diamonds in the hot sun again eh, I have told you before that a large hat was by far more useful than a kilt in this Australian sun?'

Lindsay never wore a kilt, but he never wore a bush hat either.

'I just thought you might want to know that one of your Toyota Landcruisers has been spotted in thick bush, and has not moved in a week. Got anybody missing that we should be looking for out there? We can't land the chopper as the bush is too thick, but it's certainly one of yours, as it has an orange roof, with a large number four on it.'

What luck, this was the very Landcruiser hired out to Bill Wentworth, my bright orange roof-paint has paid off yet again, Lindsay's prospecting crew has located the missing Toyota, but where did they find this vehicle?

'Yes Lindsay, we do actually have a missing Toyota; however, the people who had hired it are all safe, and now back home in New South Wales, watching TV and eating cucumber sandwiches. Where did you say the location of the vehicle was?'

'I didn't, but it's about twenty-five kilometres due north of the Great Northern Highway, and around seventy kilometres this side of Halls Creek. The Toyota appears to be on an old survey track as we can see a defined but overgrown track in the bush. But that still puts it in the middle of nowhere my wee Scottish comrade.'

This was worrying news as Lindsay might joke around, but he was usually spot-on and very experienced when it came to judging bush driving situations. If he said remote then it was a remote place, and obviously well off the normal geo exploration tracks. Lindsey was curious at this odd situation, and quite rightfully wanted to know more about this Toyota.

'Did you say the driver is okay and back in Kununurra, why was the Toyota left in the bush, who was the hirer, and why were they driving it down that old survey track? I do hope they were not the opposition spying on us laddie?'

'Oh my dear, lots of questions to answer there Lindsay, most of which I don't know the answers to yet. However, I will know more when I get my Toyota back. Nevertheless I can tell you in all honesty that they were not an opposition exploration company. You have nothing to worry about regarding spying, they were just two silly old tourists who have missed out on killing themselves.'

'Well in that case you're in luck there Jock Niven, as we have a ground crew who are just about to cut their way through on a prospecting job, from the Gibb River road to Halls Creek. I'll get them to divert a little to the right and tow your Toyota back to Halls Creek for you. It will cost you two cartoons of beer for the lads.'

'It's a done deal Lindsay; out of interest did your helicopter pilot see any other sign of life around the vehicle? The guy who hired the vehicle was Senator Bill Wentworth. He was travelling with his wife on a visit to the Kalumburu Mission. He had me convinced that he was an experienced out-back vehicle driver, reckons that he has driven many times in remote areas, and knows how to handle a four wheel drive vehicle in the bush.'

There was a low groan down the phone from my friendly Scottish Geo, then a gentle chuckle.

'Stuffing haggis man, I'll tell you what Jock, if it's the same Bill Wentworth who was the recent Federal Minister for Aboriginal Affairs. Well then I think it's a pity that the old bastard didn't bleach his bones out in the bush.

He's the silly old bugger that has been working diligently with my hard-earned tax dollars to get what he calls equal rights for the Aboriginals. He's against any mining exploration, or development in remote areas. Especially those that do not include some sort of hefty payment to "them," the Aboriginal Legal Aid lawyers who stir-up the local Aboriginal people.

It's cost my company many hundreds of thousands of dollars fighting him every step of the way. Hell, he was supposed to be on our side... a blue-chip Liberal party man.'

Oh dear, it looks like I have caused a stir. Lindsay thought all he had to worry about was some other opposition mining company sniffing around the bush close to his prospecting patch. He was most likely going to have a good look at my stranded Toyota anyway. No doubt to see if there was some clue as to what they were doing out there, or more likely for what they were looking for.

I had no idea who this Wentworth bloke was. Now Lindsey was fuming at the thought that another Aboriginal sympathiser and activist had been roaming around in the Kimberley stirring up anti exploration and mining sentiment.

'Lindsay my tartan friend calm down or you'll pee your kilt. Senator Bill is really a nice guy, he was just saying goodbye to all his Aboriginal friends on his retirement from politics. And no doubt all his expenses were paid for by your tax money that's all... no harm done old chap. Come over to my office and take a wee dram o my single malt whisky, you'll feel much better.'

How wrong I was on that particular issue, as Bill Wentworth continued to fight for indigenous Australians rights long after he left parliament. Bill was a committed and dedicated man to causes that mattered to him.

I attempted to phone Senator Bill with the news that we had found the missing Toyota, but he would not take any of my calls. I had little option than to leave a message with his solicitor who was insistent that I only contact them in writing on this matter. Therefore, in writing I advised that when the vehicle was back in my workshops and the complete damage assessed.

They would indeed be hearing from me again, and in writing, this being a full detailed account for all the costs to bring this vehicle back to a functioning hire vehicle again.

A few days later Lindsay had left a message at my office. It was advising that my Toyota Landcruiser was now in the Halls Creek Police Station security yard. In large print, Lindsey politely reminded me that I now owed him two cartoons of cold beer... Now we had another bush job for our Mr Bill Gump.

I went down to the workshop and brought Pedro up-to-date with the current details of the missing Toyota. A phone call to the Kununurra flight service advised me, Shaun Murphy of H-Cat aviation had just filed a flight plan for Halls Creek. They would get Shaun to give me a call if he had two spare seats on his aircraft.

Within half an hour Bill and the young apprentice mechanic Joe were on their way, flying to Halls Creek with a spare Toyota radiator and tools. Two hours later I took a phone call from Bill Gump; he was in good spirits, and not at all his usual miserable self.

'Hi boss, did you say you thought this Toyota had a radiator leak... you were right, it's got a bloody great tree-trunk rammed through the middle of it? The burnt pointed stub of a six-inch thick tree has gone through the radiator core and stripped off all the fan blades and ripped off the fanbelt. What do you want me to do with it?'

'Hell this sounds more serious than I had thought, Bill, can you buy a new fan blade and belt from the local BP garage and get the vehicle going again?'

There was a worrying pause, then Bill started his happy chat again.

'Didn't I tell you about the engine boss... it's seized solid, won't budge. Oh yeah and both the rear and the front drive shafts have been removed and are in the back of the tray because the transfer box has blown-up and seized. Both shafts were removed, otherwise the Stockdale boys couldn't have towed the bloody thing into Halls Creek.'

None of this was sounding very good at all, although Bill Gump was having a good time telling me all about this tragedy… and sadly there was more to come.

'Bill is there anything that can be done other than trucking the bloody thing back to Kununurra?'

'Nope, the local cops reckon I should try getting the Toyota on the back of a truck. I'm just on my way down to the Halls Creek pub now to find a truck driver who might be able to help us out.'

Christ, I thought to myself, Bill Gump going down the pub; he can't go into a pub without filling up on booze. Then I thought, well this should not be such a problem now as he will be in the truck and not driving my Toyota.

Then I thought, hang on a minute. Bill also said something about a damaged transfer box. Just then another mysterious thought came to me, a thick steel belly plate always protects this part. Bill Gump quickly came fourth with a question and the answer in bubbling excitement.

'Boss do you know what happens to a mechanical power winch when some stupid fucker replaces the normal shaft sheer-pin with a six-inch nail? Yes that's right, the winch is much more powerful than the PTO (power take-off) of the transfer case, and the case just explodes under the immense torque and strain.'

It was nice to hear that Bill Gump was in a happy mood for a change, maybe we should have a few more Toyota Landcruiser disasters to cheer him up. There was another short pause and then Bill passed on his parting news.

'Boss, you haven't asked me what caused the power winch to fail.'

I was still too shocked at the amount of damage to answer. Without any prompting Bill continued his story in a cheerful voice.

'Well you know how the lazy bastards are to winch in the steel cable back onto the drum after use. Yeah that's right they just wrap the bloody excess cable all around the bull-bar. When this Senator bloke drove off with the winch leaver still engaged, it pulled the heavy steel winch rope tightly around the bull-bar.

Collapsing the whole bloody bull-bar into a tight twisted bent mess, all because the shiny new six inch nail used as a winch shear-pin wouldn't shear. Of course this all stopped when the PTO (power take-off) on the transfer case blew-up, we'll have to cut this bloody lot off with an oxy torch when I get back. With a bit-of-luck we should see you back in Kununurra in about six hour's'

Yes well, as it turned, out Bill did need more than just a bit-of-luck on that day; however, I could not stop thinking about this whole strange scenario...

How could this be, a slightly built little man and his frail wife, both in their early seventies. Senator Bill being an old retired city slicker politician had with little effort just managed to reduce my eight-month-old Toyota Landcruiser four wheel drive vehicle into a scrap heap in just six weeks.

The Senator had wrecked this vehicle to almost a write-off in a casual drive around the Australian bush. He had broken-down in a very remote place, then he and his frail wife, on foot, walked for five hours through rough desert scrub under the hot tropical sun. Eventually by some amazing measure of luck to stagger out onto a two-lane highway and thumb down a passing truck. Just what were the odds on surviving that grim situation?

It was now eleven o'clock, so all going well we should see Bill and Joe back at around five this afternoon, and we did, well Pedro did. Bill Gump had rang Pedro from the Mobil truck-stop, which is about twelve kilometres out of town, that was as far as the truckie that helped Bill would go that day. Seemingly by Pedro's description, Bill Gump was in one of the worst psycho states he had ever seen him in; he was literarily off his brain.

By all accounts, Joe, the young Aboriginal apprentice mechanic was not much better, he had disappeared well before Pedro had arrived at the Mobil truck-stop to bring them both back into town. Bill was not very coherent and was babbling an amazing story, so Pedro just took Bill home, got him into bed with a rum and coke and left. The frightening and unbelievable story eventually told the next day.

Apparently Bill Gump could not find a truck going to Kununurra with enough space on the back for the Toyota. On the other hand, a very drunk truck driver had offered to tow the Toyota all the way back to Kununurra... all three hundred and sixty kilometres.

After another hour in the pub trying to find a truck, Bill was then left with no other option but to accept the tow offer. All was ready with Bill Gump steering the Toyota and Joe in the passenger seat, they set off for a non-stop drive to Kununurra.

Bill had completely forgotten that Toyota brakes have no power assistance without the engine running, and no engine breaking assistance with the tail shaft removed...

Of course this was not possible anyhow, as the engine had seized up solid. He was soon to learn that his biggest problem was the pissed truck driver, who forgot that he was towing the Toyota. Bill Gump reckoned that on the trip back to Kununurra the truck rarely went below ninety kilometres an hour.

He really had no exact idea just how fast they were going, as the tail-shaft that drives the speedometer on the Toyota was in the back tray of the vehicle. However, he did know from considerable mad driving experience that it was fast.

Many times the truck braked hard to slow down for a bend or another vehicle. This caused the Toyota to catch up with the truck slamming hard into the rear trailer, as the Toyota had no power brakes and no hope of slowing down in time. When the truck accelerated again, this caused the heavy tow-chain to extend to its maximum length with an almighty neck snapping jolt.

Much as they tried they could not gain the driver's attention. The truck just continued on at a reckless speed down the narrow sealed highway. The other terrifying thing was the fear of running over the slack tow-chain after the truck had slowed down.

Bill Gump knew if this were to happen it would easily rip off a front-wheel and flip the Toyota over. In that event, the powerful Mac truck would most likely have just driven on, dragging the Toyota like a fallen horse rider caught in a stirrup, until the tow-chain finally snapped.

Bill was giving this terrifying situation his maximum attention, while constantly keeping the slack tow-chain between the Toyota front wheels. With all of this going on and trying to avoid smashing into the rear of the truck for a long terrifying four hours, the strain had taken its toll on poor Bill's brain.

Personally think Bill did a fine job in staying alive for that long. Was this another example of Bill Gump's good survival luck again... who knows... who would bloody know?

What a mess. My first view of the hire Toyota was as it first came into the yard, towed by Pedro and Greg. The damaging burnt tree stump still firmly lodged in the front of the vehicle. I noticed other scrub-bush material tightly wrapped around the tree stump and the front grill. All indicating to me, this vehicle had travelled for some distance through the bush, after the tree stump staked the radiator.

The sides of the Toyota had many dents and deeply scratched, again telling me that the vehicle had been "scrub bashing," a term describing when a vehicle is used as a battering ram through thick wooded scrub to make its own road.

I then noticed that the windscreen had a number of large cracks and a considerable amount of stone damage, thinking this would have made driving very difficult. Thinking this obstructed view would have been an absolutely terrifying experience for Bill Gump, towed at about ninety kilometres an hour, for over four hours.

Both the spare wheels were flat; with the tyres staked through, and now beyond any possible repair. This was one of the worst cases of vehicle abuse I had seen in my many years in the vehicle hire business. Pedro was disgusted at the level of damage and asked me to take a look at the mess underneath the vehicle.

The heavy steel transmission protection plate was bent and buckled, and all four leaf springs were broken. The complete exhaust system was missing, obviously ripped off in the bush. I was thinking to myself what sort of hell Bill Gump and Joe would have gone through yesterday, when I heard Bill speak. He was standing right behind me.

'Number four's in a right fucking mess boss but we'll have her all fixed up and back on the road in a week. That's assuming that the seized engine hasn't cracked the engine block.'

Bill Gump had recovered quickly; he looked tired but still had the same deadpan expressionless look on his face. This terrifying experience did not fuss this tough (if not a little dim) mechanic in the slightest, his only concern now was to get this Toyota fixed-up and ready for hire again.

'Are you sure you're feeling okay Bill,' this lot, waving my arms at the broken Toyota, 'can wait for a day or two. I can't begin to imagine how terrifying it must have been for you being towed by that truck yesterday.'

Bill Gump looked down at his well-worn steel-capped dessert boots and mumbled like a naughty little boy giving his truthful reply.

'That crazy tow back to Kununurra was probably mostly my fault Boss. I was drinking in the pub with the truck-driver until he was pissed out of his mind, then I agreed to be towed back to Kununurra. I should know better, forgetting that a Toyota has no power brakes without the engine running.'

Sadly looking up at me he said.

'It's a wonder I didn't kill myself, we certainly came close to it a few times, if it wasn't for young Joe being with me...'

I quickly cut Bill off in midsentence as I felt that he may be about to speak on something that I really didn't want to hear anything about. Then I quickly changed the subject.

'By the way where is Joe, he hasn't turned up for work today and it's his payday, now that's not like Joe to miss his pay?'

Bill Gump looked out through the workshop door into the vehicle holding yard, and casually remarked.

'He's probably gone on walk-about again, we might not see him for a long-time, can't really blame him after what he went through yesterday.'

Bill Gump was referring to the time when Joe, being a full blood Aboriginal just disappeared one day. This was shortly after we had managed to get him a mechanics apprenticeship.

A full year later Joe just turned-up for work one morning, dressed in his company tee-shirt and work boots... just as if nothing had happened. His once boyish charm had all gone.

Joe looked a good ten years older complete with what may have been knife scars down one side of his now hard face. I asked Joe where he had been all this time. He just hunched his shoulders and quietly said he had been on walk-about and went back to working on a vehicle alongside Greg, and that was that.

The damage account was staggering. On close examination Bill Gump was right about the engine block it was cracked, and so was the cylinder head. Both were now throwaway items along with the smashed transfer casing and most of the spring leaves.

As promised, I sent a full account for all the repair work to Senator Bill. A battle of legal threats started, the man refusing to acknowledge any responsibility for the damage he caused. He then eventually reluctantly agreed to pay half of the account, declaring the offer was on what he called "as a gesture of goodwill."

Senator Bill sent a cheque for half the account stating that if I cashed his cheque. I had then agreed to his terms, and could make no further claims from him regarding this matter of the hired Toyota.

I had some long and painful thoughts over this pittance of an offer. However in the end decided to accept the cheque, as this would have most certainly ended up as a long drawn-out protracted court case. No doubt with some law expert friend of Senator Bill directing the symphony in the eastern states of Australia over three thousand kilometres away.

One bright thing happened though... Joe turned up for work eight months later. He said nothing and just went back to work alongside Greg on another broken Toyota; however, he was never again to be the same Joe we once knew.

Chapter: Sixteen.

Keep trying until you succeed

Another seven weeks went by, it was now early December, and the first signs of a big tropical monsoon season were there for all to see. This was the time of the year known to the locals in Kununurra as the "Troppo season" when normal people that you knew quite well went a little strange, said strange things, did strange things.

One would notice these odd changes making no comment, just a silent understanding in mutual sympathy. This was the time of the year of high temperatures, bringing intolerable heavy humidity with shimmering bitumen road heat. At this time of the year you can't avoid the searing hot air that you must breathe, or the things that you can't avoid touching, like a vehicle door handle.

As yet, there was no relief from any of the promised rain, held in the massive build-ups of black cumulus clouds that gathered every afternoon. These were regular cloud formations that would mysteriously all disappear in the night to a clear morning sky.

Everyone complained that his or her air-conditioning just wasn't working. When in reality, the truth of the matter was that the air-con units installed were working well beyond their designed subtropical capacity. As such were struggling to provide any form of relief to their hopeful owners.

Nothing but nothing made by man could handle this zero breeze, still air, inland heavy tropical climate.

I was standing in the cave-bar replacing my rapidly declining body liquid, and trying to concentrate on a simple conversation with a friend.

The bar air-conditioning was not coping. I could see the beer that he was consuming, pour out of his skin in the form of sweat, almost as fast as he was drinking the amber liquid. In these extreme hot times, even I would turn to the greater fluid advantage of beer. Foregoing my usual drink of rum and coke.

This was not a happy time of the year since just about all of the local business income suffered badly. The tourists stayed away, while the locals flew south to enjoy the southern summer, and by now all the farmers had finished their cropping for the year.

Mining and exploration companies were winding down their operations for the three month wet season, busy paying off their casual work force. For most people, who had the means, they had packed-up and headed south to enjoy the glorious Australian summer.

They would simply stay away, to wait out the uncomfortable wet season in the tropics. All except for the hard-core few.

Those were the few left behind as skeleton staff. The ones who would look after property and stock. And of course all those who could not afford to travel, or maybe those who had no family reasons to join the migration south... Bill Gump was one of those people.

All our attempts at finding a woman for Bill were proving unsuccessful to date. The chance of achieving any hope to resolving "Operation First Fuck" was rapidly diminishing. As was the large number of the town's population who had now departed for their pleasant summer in the south.

However, not all of the Kununurra residents wanted to flee south. Many looked upon this time of the year as the low-stress party time, but before the parties could start the wet season had to start. The torrential monsoonal rains had to start falling to bring-down the oppressive heat; heat that would instantly exchange the high temperatures for an equally oppressive high humidity. At least it was a weather change. Therefore this was the critical time, a time just before the wet started, and a critical time for one's own sanity.

Pedro had been talking to Morrie at the pub about his stock car, about how well it was doing in the finals when the conversation drifted over to Bill and his unhappy depressive state.

Morrie was a bit concerned at some of the things that Bill would say, while working on his stock car out at Dessert Seeds. He would argue about the silliest little things, especially on how the car was to be set-up for the next race meeting and so on. He had also noticed that Bill had developed a worrying infatuation with Robyn; Morrie's nice looking wife, and to him, this was now becoming a concern.

The monsoon season was getting to everyone this year, including Morrie. I just wished the skies would open-up and the rain thunder down, that would fix almost all of the problems in Kununurra at this moment... except Bill Gump's personal problems.

It was a Saturday, I had finished my office work for the day. From around one o'clock until five was my quiet time of the week, a time to catch-up on all the paperwork that I had managed to avoid during the working week. Now it was time for a quick drink at the pub before going home to Lesley and the kids.

The cave bar was almost empty; standing all alone at the bar was Keith Wrong the local pharmacist. He was dressed in his long Caftan, well engrossed in downing another large cold beer.

'Hi Keith very quiet in here today I guess in this heat everybody is at home trying to stay cool.'

Keith wiped the froth from his mouth with his Caftan and replied firmly.

'Most of the town's people have gone down south for the wet. I think they are all missing out on the best time of the year in Kununurra. Are you going to Perth this wet?'

Keith was one of those blokes that would look at things differently and apply the most practical solution, and this was yet another example. He had just recently returned from an overseas holiday. Deciding that the best and most practical way to keep cool in this heat was to adopt the style of clothing used in other hot countries, for example the Caftan.

Keith was most probably correct, considering this searing hot uncomfortable climate. On the other hand, none of the blokes in Kununurra were game to take him up on his Caftan example. I liked Keith, he was more than just the local pharmacist he could, and would, turn his hand to just about anything. He was not the usual soft image of a pharmacist, but a tough kind of wiry guy that had worked in a number of manual jobs. He knew his way around a bulldozer, flying aeroplanes, driving trucks, and running a nightclub; and yes, drinking booze and enjoying himself.

In other words, a man of out-back commitment and vision, yet still a typical town character. For me, maybe not a man that I would follow, (Caftan included.) Nevertheless, most certainly a smart man that I would give some time to listen too.

I ordered my drink and sat down for a casual chat with Keith, whose current projects were building a house, and finishing the modification and fit-out of his new pharmacy. All of which he did almost single-handed. I gave Keith an honest answer.

'Yeah I will be going down to Perth for Christmas, but I'll be back in early January, so I'll still be here for most of the wet season. Lesley and the kids will stay down a bit longer. It will give them a nice break, and they can see all the family again.'

I was not game to venture down the path of Keith's family. A man never enquires or asks such things during a drink in the North-West. They will tell you if they feel inclined to at some stage... or maybe never.

'You're new pharmacy is coming along well, it looks almost finished, will you open this year, or early January?'

I had moved to a subject that Keith could talk about all day, he responded with his usual enthusiasm.

'The new pharmacy will be open by this time next week, in fact I have to go meet the Perth jet at six thirty to pick-up my new pharmacy assistant. That's why I have taken the trouble to get dressed-up a little.'

Keith gave a robe display by twirling his Caftan, then added a little chuckle, and resumed drinking. I thought holy shit, trying to visualise this coming meeting at the airport. Keith in his flowing Caftan saying "hello I'm your new boss, follow me out to the Ute,"... just then Pedro walked into the bar with a worried look on his face and strode up to the bar where Keith and I was sitting. Without even a glance at Keith clad in his odd Caftan, he spilled out his concern.

'He's gone and done it again, Bill's trying to bleeding write himself off again.'

Pedro was visually upset, but Keith had the immediate answer.

'I'll get you a beer to settle you down a bit Pedro, anyway, how do you know that Bill is trying it on again, I thought he was over all that kind of stuff.'

Pedro shifted his attention to Keith at the same time his worried look turned to an authentic look of surprise.

'What in the bleeding hell is that dress you've got on, you look like my aunt Betty on a bad day at the Bingo... hey, are you wearing any underpants with that?'

Keith was not amused at Pedro's humourist observation of his new tropical attire.

'It's a Caftan you ignorant fucker, it's a-lot cooler than the gear that you've got on. Here drink your bloody beer and tell us what's happened to that silly bastard Bill?'

Pedro took a large swig of the beer leaving half for his next go, wiped his mouth with the back of his hand, and proceeded to us all that he knew.

'I've just left talking with Morrie. Bill was out at Morrie's place all day drinking and working on the speedway car for tomorrow night's big race. Apparently, he all of a sudden got into one hell of an argument with Morrie about which differential they should install for tonight's race meeting. Bill insisted on the 3 point 55 and Morrie wanted to fit the 4 point 44 then Bill....'

Keith being a man of little patience and flowing robes briskly interjected.

'For fucks sake man, get on with it. Who cares a fuck about that crappy speedway car... what the hell happened to Bill Gump?'

Pedro looked a bit miffed at being cut-off at the knees on the important detail of his story, but reluctantly continued.

'Well, Bill's been spending a fair bit of time at Morrie's house chatting with Morrie's wife Robyn. Morrie being a right jealous bastard was in the middle of accusing Bill of trying to get into Robyn's pants, just as she came over to the workshop with another couple of beers. Robyn had managed to split them up before they came to blows, and that's when he said it.'

Pedro licked his lips and reached out to retrieve his remaining half glass of beer from the bar when suddenly Keith let fly with a salvo of verbal abuse.

'Jesus you make me bloody mad Pedro... he said what for fucks sake, spit it out?'

Pedro was most surprised at Keith's urgent demand for a conclusion to his story. Kimberley protocol does give a man the right to consume his first beer in peace. Pedro thought it best to comply with Keith's request and continued his story.

'He said that was it. There was no point in living anymore and reckoned this time he knew just how to do it, and then he stormed out. Apparently Robyn chased after him, pleading with him to calm down, and Bill telling them all to get stuffed.

Morrie came over to tell me about what had happened so the first thing we did was go over to Bill's caravan. Bill wasn't at home but we noticed that he had brought back the hire vehicle and parked it back on the line. Morrie and Robyn have gone out looking in all the likely places to try to find him, and I came over to find you.'

This was not sounding good at all. The worrying thought was that Bill had put-up with a considerable amount of ridicule down at the pub over his last attempt at resolving all his problems. Most of the local drunks thought it helpful, by suggesting a number of ingenious methods to do the deed. Bill had accepted the amusing remarks as just pub humour, but how much is too much. He was now missing and presumed on a suicide mission, now with a head full of new ideas... We needed a plan of action.

There was little point in us all looking in the same place. We did have one small advantage as both Pedro's and my Ute were fitted with CB radios so we could keep in touch with each other during the search.

'Pedro any ideas on what Bill might try this time. I mean he's all out of vehicles and has returned the Toyota hire vehicle, which means that he is most likely on foot, that must limit his opportunities a bit, don't you think?'

Staring at his now empty beer glass Pedro looked a little guilty, then he hunched his shoulders and I just knew he was about to confess something.

'Well, I feel a bit ashamed to say it, but the last time Bill tried to knock himself off, I suggested that he should give-up on motor cars, as they had all proved useless and try something different. He did ask what and, well, I figured that since he couldn't swim he should try drowning himself. He agreed with me and said it would be a nice clean way to go... but I don't think he meant clean, clean if you know what I mean.'

Then Keith came alive with loud determination.

'Whose shout is it? This is a bloody dry rescue mission; we'll all die of dehydration before we can save Bill.' Then as an afterthought, 'I didn't know Bill couldn't swim, the blokes been trying to drown himself with booze ever since I've known him.'

I thought to myself, Keith may well be right about that, but drowning in water would be an unlikely choice for Bill, after all he is British. Then again you never know, desperate times calls for desperate measures, and this hot weather could drive a man to anything.

I started implementing a simple search plan.

'I think we should have just one more drink then hit the road to look for Bill. Pedro, since you suggested drowning to Bill, I reckon that you should go check-out places like the Ord Diversion Dam, the swimming spot and the ski beach. Keith and I will check out all his likely drinking spots such as the Sports Club and Gulliver's Tavern. Then we will go check out all the high spots like Kelly's Knob as he might fancy jumping off something. Then the main Highway in case he decides to walk in front of a Mack truck. We can report our findings back with the CB radio, any questions?'

Keith still had a problem to resolve.

'Yeah I'll ask again, who's buying the next bloody round, and I think we're going to need a few extra stubbies for the road search.'

And so it was that memorable and sad day. With the help of a few volunteers, we soon had a group of around ten or more people who cared enough about Bill Gump and his safety to join the search. Outside, the end of the day was rapidly fading into a searing hot tropical night. We needed to move fast if we were to get to the top of Kelly's Knob before we lost all the light. The narrow road up to the tourist lookout was always a problem as you could only turn around at the top. If you were unfortunate enough to meet someone on the way down, then one vehicle would have to either back-up all the way to the top or bottom… who was the one to reverse was the one who could best convince the other… that was always interesting.

At the lookout, we could still see quite clearly over the town. Keith was the first to notice the few cigarette butts by the guardrail, stooping down in his flowing Caftan robe he picked one up and announced in an English accent like a proper Sherlock Holmes.

'I do believe that our Mr Bill Gump has been here Watson. These cigarette butts are "Menthol" and Mr Gump is the only man I know of in town who smokes that particular brand.'

I must admit I was very impressed, especially since Keith was not a smoker, and that he should know about Bill's strange habit of smoking only strong menthol cigarettes. Not to be outdone I followed his lead.

'Quite so Holmes, you have indeed discovered an important clue. Shall we inspect the likely body landing site before the light leaves us this day?'

We could see nothing of Bill from the small-elevated lookout. Keith and I then decided to climbed down to the base of the four metre rock-face after which the ground fell away into a steep slope. If Bill had thrown himself off that lookout, we would have easily seen where the landing point was. I had to keep a straight face watching Keith scrambling around amongst the rocks in his Caftan looking like an Arab Camel driver from Afghanistan picking up valuable Camel dung.

The next stop was Gulliver's Tavern, on the way I opened my mind of thoughts to my Caftan robed friend.

'If Bill has been to the Kelly's Knob lookout, how would he have got there without a vehicle, and why would he have changed his mind?'

Keith was well ahead of me with his own theory on Bill's odd movements.

'I reckon that while Bill still had the Toyota hire vehicle, he drove from the Morrie's argument at Dessert Seeds direct to the Kelly's Knob look-out. He had a few cigarettes contemplating on what he was going to do next and left to get a drink.'

'And what brings you to that conclusion Holmes?'

'Well my dear Watson, this location can only be reached by transport so Mr Bill Gump must have had access to such means. Also Mr Gump's preferred social drink is a rum and coke, by my observation my dear Watson there were no empty cans of coke at the lookout. One would then assume, considering the current ambient heat and Mr Gump's depressed state of mind that his most likely decision would have been to get a drink, possibly in an attempt to get drunk.'

This was impressive stuff coming from Keith, the logic was also quite sound... maybe I should get myself a Caftan...

At the Tavern, the barman confirmed that Bill had indeed braced his bar about two hours ago, and then we went to the bottle shop next door. We soon discovered that Bill in a bad mood, had purchased half a cartoon of coca-a-cola and a large bottle of Bundaberg rum. All this information now confirmed that Keith was indeed correct on all of his theories. Nevertheless, where the hell did he go, where was Bill now?

While in the bottle shop we had purchased another six-pack of beer, and while Keith was refilling the cooler box, the CB radio burst into life.

'Mobile two to mobile one, manager here come back.'

'Go ahead manager what have you got?'

'Target location confirmed Diversion Dam control tower. Should we call in the blue now, do you copy?'

'Copy manager, no sit tight we're on our way to your location now.'

A frightening shiver went down my spine, had Pedro found Bill in the water at the Diversion Dam, had he jumped off the control tower, should we now call in the Police? We needed to get to the Diversion Dam and quick. As I roared off towards the Diversion Dam Keith let fly with his frustration.

'What's with this shitty CB radio crap talk? I didn't understand a bloody word that Pedro was on about… has something happened?'

'Keith, we can't use plain conversation on the CB radio as every man and his dog is listening in, you see it's not very private. Pedro thinks or is sure that Bill has jumped off the Diversion Dam control tower, and is suggesting we should now call in the Police. As you know, attempted suicide in Western Australia is an offense under the law. I hope Pedro is wrong about this, but we need to be sure.'

Keith thought about what I had said, then aired his educated and expert opinion.

'I've jumped off that control tower hundreds of times, mostly when I was drunk, we all did it; it's no big deal. A thirty foot fall and a big splash isn't going to kill anyone, unless a crock gets him, and that's unlikely. He would frighten the shit out of those little Johnson crocks if he landed on one.'

'You're probably right Keith but remember that Bill can't swim, and it's very dark now.'

The remainder of the drive out to the Diversion Dam was in silence as we were both thinking about what we might find. As we passed the airport, Keith perked up a little as he remembered that he had to meet the plane to pick-up his new pharmacy assistant.

'The jet will be in at six thirty, can we call in at the airport on the way back and pick-up my new pharmacy girl?'

'Pharmacy girl, you didn't tell me your new assistant was a girl. That's real good news Keith; we could do with more girls in Kununurra, especially at this time of the year.'

Keith shot me a confused staring look of doubtful concern...'Well her names Mary so I bloody-well hope she's a girl,' then in a gruff afterthought... 'It will go back on the next plane if it's not.'

The bright lights of the Diversion Dam came into view as I picked out Pedro's Holden Ute in the small car park alongside. It was only a short walk to the control tower bridge, which was on this side of the Ord Dam crossing. Pedro, Morrie, and a few others were on the tower gantry-walk looking down into the water with powerful dauphine lantern torches.

Although frowned upon by the authorities, this was a favourite spot for the locals to have a nice view of the Dam, enjoy a few beers, and throw in a fishing line. However, at this time of the year in this heat the only people likely to be at this spot were the adventurous ones that would jump off the high gantry-deck into the water to keep cool.

As I approached the tower I recognised Pedro and quietly asked, 'found anything yet?' just then Morrie turned around and spotted Keith, gasping 'Jesus.'

Quick-as-a-flash Keith responded,

'No it's not Jesus mate, only Keith the pharmacist in a Caftan.'

Nobody laughed as the mood of the searchers was serious and not open to any humour, then Pedro spoke and saved the fragile moment.

'We've found some menthol cigarette butts and some empty coke cans the very garbage that only Bill would leave. We think he's jumped from here.'

Keith and I were not convinced. Keith borrowed a dauphine lantern torch and started poking around; meanwhile I gave my views to the others on the situation.

'The way Keith and I have things figured out. Bill in his shitty mood then drove from Morrie's place to the top of Kelly's Knob to consider things over in his mind for a while, because we also found some of Bill's menthol butts up there. He then went to Gulliver's Tavern and had a few drinks, bought a bottle of Bundy rum and some cans of coke from the bottle-shop, and then drove home. He then parked up the Toyota hire vehicle at work, and from there he walked to somewhere.'

Morrie responded with what he thought was the obvious.

'He probably hiked a lift out here with his booze, had a few rum and cokes, and then jumped in the Ord River.'

This didn't sound right to me. For a start, Bill would have finished off the bottle of rum first before jumping into the Dam. Bill would not have wasted any rum by leaving some behind. Then Keith spoke.

'These coke cans have been bleached by the sun and the cigarette butts are rock-hard. I'd say they've been here for weeks, possibly since last time Bill had contemplated an attempt at Hara Kari. It looks like he chickened out leaving all his bloody garbage behind again.

I kept forgetting that Keith was on the Kununurra tourism committee and one of his pet subjects was about keeping the town clean, and then came a sigh from Pedro.

'Looks like we're back to square one, where do we look next?'

Keith and I could see the next move, and we would need to hurry.

'Listen you guy's wherever Bill is, it's within walking distance of Gulliver's Tavern; just how far could you walk carrying half a cartoon of coke and a large bottle of rum. My only worry is that when he has finished the rum, that's when he will do himself in. It's been over two hours since he bought the booze so I guess the question is, how long will it take Bill to finish off the large bottle of rum?'

There was a long silence as the mob of helpers digested all this relevant and new information, then someone in the dark piped-up.

'What are you blokes, some sort of Sherlock fucking Holmes or what?'

Keith being a man of little tolerance or patience for stupid remarks, unless the comments were intended as funny, responded by jumping down the heckler's throat.

'Who cares a-stuff if we're playing at Sherlock Holmes, the fact is we have worked out what Bill is doing and approximately where he is. He's got to be within walking distance of the bloody Tavern. We should all split-up and head for any likely spot that offers a possible way for him to kill himself, and any place he might get his hands-on a gun....'

Everyone looked at Keith with a dumb expression, including me.

'That's right you idiots a bloody gun, it's about the only way he hasn't fucking tried yet!'

I quickly recovered from this more than obvious choice of departing this world. Composing myself, added my bit in the form of a stirring speech.

'Friends, time is now running out for Bill. While Keith was blasting you lot with some common sense, I have figured out Bills timeline. Having already drunk a fair bit of booze today, and knowing his mighty tolerance for alcohol. I would go as far as to say that the rum would be just about all gone by now, there-for his time is almost up. We all need to get going right now, and find Bill.'

The rescue crowd headed for their vehicles and back into town. Keith and I headed for the airport just as the Perth jet flight had gone overhead. The Fokker Fellowship was unloading it's passengers as we pulled-up in the car park.

Not many people arrive to stay at this time of the year; however, there were quite a number of locals on their way to the Eastern states via Darwin.

Keith striding around in his Caftan drew a considerable amount of comment and attention, which didn't bother Keith one little bit.

As was normal all the passengers travelling through to Darwin and the Eastern states tended to get off the plane and stretch their legs and have a smoke, so it was a bit difficult to work-out who was staying and who was going on to Darwin.

Looking around there was a number of women on the flight that might have fitted Keith's description if I knew what that was. Then turning to Keith...

'Keith, how will you know just who your new pharmacy assistant is out of this lot?' Waving my arms around in the general direction of the large group of chatting passengers...

Just then a very unsteady looking woman in her early thirties stumbled towards me sporting a quaint but strained smile. She obviously thought I had signalled or waved at her to come over to me.

'Hello my names Mary, you must be Keith Wrong the pharmacist. Gee it's bloody hot up here and that was a long bloody flight. I had no idea how faraway Kununurra was until now, it certainly doesn't look all that far on the small map I have.'

Mary had obviously had many drinks on her long flight to Kununurra, no doubt to while away the time. Keith and I were silently studying Mary she was not too bad looking, I guess with an 8½ out of 10 figure and a nice smile. Just then, a loud voice boomed out, "luggage and freight, over here;" then with a girly giggle, she suddenly turned and headed for the freight trolley. Keith had a sly smile on his face. I suspected that he had assembled some sort of mischief.

'I suppose I don't look much like a pharmacist in this?' posing in his Caftan, arms outspreaded with palms facing up, looking very pious and stately.

'No you look like a bloody a bad effigy of Jesus Christ or an Arab Camel driver without a Camel.'

'Niven, how about you introduce me to Mary as your Arab friend.'

Now I see Keith almost every day, so it does not occur to me that he sports a considerable suntan from his many hours working on outside jobs. Many others and I had become use to Keith and his rather odd ways, so standing next to Keith in a Caftan doesn't bother me at all. However, this must have looked a bit out of place, or strange for a newcomer such as Mary. She was about to become the victim of some north-west humour and local education.

We both followed Mary across to the freight trolley and I collected her suitcases, while Keith stood back as any well bread Arab Prince would, and let me do all the work.

'Mary, please allow me to introduce you to His Highness Prince Keff Dus-noall, son of King-sound and Heir to the Land Rover near Webber Plains.'

Keith took a stately bow, his caftan billowing nicely in the light tropical breeze then taking Mary's hand spoke in his best Arabic accent.

'Madam I am honoured to meet you. May my large pleasure soon be your pleasure, and may your pleasures, be mine one day.'

A small delay ensued as both Mary and I tried to decipher just what Keith meant by that last comment. Then with a well-timed pause and a scholarly look he continued.

'Perhaps sometime soon you may wish to join me for lunch on my small yacht or possibly a flight over the Ord River irrigation system in my private aircraft?'

Mary was most impressed at this offer, especially as it was only her first few minutes in Kununurra. As I remembered, Keith's boat was an eight-foot long battered fishing tinnie that had not been in the water for years. This leaky little boat, presently used as a cover to keep his cement bags dry. On the other hand, Keith did have a very nice new Cessna 182 aircraft that I have hired from time to time. Then it all happened. One of the loudmouth locals, topped-up with an abundance of going away on holiday booze, spotted Keith in his flowing Caftan.

'Keith you look like a bloody poofter in that dress, don't you feel like a bleeding idiot. You look lovely, but don't bloody bend over too far mate.

Caught off guard by this surprise attack, Keith let his excellent Arab disguise slip, responding to the drunk in a loud threatening voice.

'Get fucking stuffed Magpie, I know you've always fancied me. Any more crap out of you and I'll tell your missus all about Leon your painter boyfriend and that last bout of the clap that you needed my pharmacy for.'

Magpie the painter wished he had kept his big mouth shut. Pity those who attempt to cross verbal swords with the wit and considerable local knowledge of Keith Wrong.

Mary quickly caught on to our bit of fun, and we were both pleased and relieved that Mary had a great sense of humour. This being the most important qualification required to survive in the north-west. Mary apologised for being slightly pissed, as she had fallen asleep on the plane for three out of the five hour flight-time, but was willing to catch-up, so Keith handed her a cold beer.

I was thinking Keith was lucky to find an employee like Mary. We had only known Mary for a few minutes. Yet she had already displayed many of the finer qualities for becoming a permanent Kununurra resident.

As we lifted Mary's suitcases on to the back of the ute the CB radio came alive again with Pedro saying that nobody had anything good to report but were all still looking. Since we had proved to be the best detectives, could we do a bit more detective work urgently as time was running out fast to save Bill?

Mary asked what that was all about, so Keith quickly told Mary the story about Bill being very depressed and suicidal. Adding that we were all worried he might try harming himself, well actually commit suicide. Mary couldn't understand why he would want to do something like that, so I told her a little about Bill.

'Bill is one of the nicest guys I ever known, he would do anything to help anyone, he gives up his time to assist in many of the town events. If you need any help Bill will always be there to lend a helping hand. Mind you, (I quickly added) Bill is not without his faults. He drinks a lot, swears a lot, and has one hell-of-a-temper but I don't think anybody could ever say that Bill is a fighting man. He's never hurt anyone, well not intentionally; he's just too nice a bloke.

Most people take advantage of Bills easy going generosity, and Bill thinks they are his friends.'

I glanced at Mary as I was driving along and noticed the puzzled look on her face, and then she replied with a giggle.

'You've just described to me… the almost perfect man.'

'Almost perfect man?' I enquired.

'Well except for the temper bit and the depression.'

'Yes you do have a point there, however if Bill were in the right kind of relationship I am certain that both of those two minor faults would be resolved and quickly disappear. You see the main problem is that Bill has never experienced a woman in his life. If he had... well none of this would have ever happened.'

Mary was now taking a deep interest in our friend Bill, and his problems, the questions just kept coming.

'Surely this Bill must have a Mother, how old is this man, and he must have had a girlfriend before?'

Keith as impatient as ever, and not one known to mince words, cut to the chase with a brutal thrust of male explanation.

'For Christ sake Mary, Niven doesn't mean about Bill not having a Mother or friendly girl in his life, he means that Bill has never had a fuck in his life, he's a bloody twenty five-year-old fuckless virgin.'

I just had to steal a look across at Mary; she was more fascinated than amazed... Keith's very descriptive verbal communication did not upset her one bit.

'Are you two guys saying that to save this man's life, all he has to have is some experience with a woman in bed?'

I caught a glimpse of Keith; he was taking an unusual interest in this conversation. The new smirk on his face had me worried... he then snapped.

'Yup that's about it in a nut-shell, if he could fuck his brains out just the once he would then most likely become a normal bloke, just like me and Niven.'

There was a short pause in Mary's torrent of questions. Keith and I sensed that Mary was about to make an important statement, or was it an announcement.

'Well, I will tell you guys right now, if that's all it would take to save this man's life, then I would make myself available to provide such a service.'

If silence was golden, then there was ten ton of gold in the front of that Ute that night, both Keith and I were speechless.

We had not even reached the turn-off into the town entry from the airport, and now we had the answer in our grasp to resolve all of Bill's problems. However, Keith was a little more cautious than I was, and moved into his serious councillor speech voice.

'Mary, in carrying out this generous offer you would be fixing up all Bill's life-long problems, but I must make you aware of our strict Kimberley code of ethics, and that number one on that list is.

"Never make a promise that you don't intend to keep."

'If Bill survives this night, then Niven and I will expect you to keep your promise.'

Mary never turned her head and just kept looking out the windscreen onto the dark road ahead. Sounding more like reciting her marriage vows, than repeating her offer. Mary slowly replied...

'I do this day promise to keep my promise to satisfy this guy Bill in bed if it will help save this man's life...' Then quickly added, 'but he has got to be alive.'

Both Keith and I looked at each other, not altogether sure what Mary meant or intended by that last bit and put it down to the alcohol. I shook my head and came out of my stunned composure almost missing the turn-off into the town.

All of a sudden the CB radio blurted out again startling us, Pedro's excited voice spilt out a torrent of words, they had found Bill. He had tried sneaking back into the Tavern bottle-shop to buy another bottle of Bundy rum, since he still had a fair bit of coke a cola left. He was spotted by one of the search crew and held down by three of the big blokes.

Bill was not at all happy at this aggressive interruption, as it had ruined his final solution plan, a plan to which he later confessed. Apparently, Bill had spent most of the time sitting up on the top of Mount Cyril, which just happens to be directly opposite where Keith and I live on Webber Plains Road.

Bill was somewhat amused at watching all the vehicles below whizzing about as everybody was out searching for him. He was planning to get totally blotto and out-of-his-mind and then jump off the other side of Mount Cyril, which just happened to have a shear drop of three hundred feet down into Hidden Valley.

Keith reckoned that was quite slick thinking on Bill's part, as that's where the local Kununurra cemetery was, and it would have only have been a short trip to a permanent hole in the ground.

Pedro had taken Bill home to his caravan, deciding to keep a close eye on him and was going to stay with him all night. Pedro would catch-up with me in the morning.

It had now gone two in the morning when I dropped Keith off at his new house; a house that he had built (correction) was building himself. Mary was going to stay there for a few days until she got herself sorted out with some local accommodation.

I left them both in deep conversation, arguing over the fact that the bedroom Keith had arranged for Mary had no door. Keith pointed out that there were no internal doors as yet fitted in his new house. However, the problem was quickly resolved; apparently, Keith was going to fit Mary's bedroom with a nice new door before she went to bed.

Bill lived in a small caravan in the backyard of his workplace Multi Agencies. When I arrived at work that Sunday morning, Peter and Bill were sitting on two canvas folding chairs on the concrete hardstand, an area used as a car wash-down bay, both drinking large cups of strong black coffee.

The hot coffee was odd considering the forty-two degree heat outside, then again my guess was that Pedro, and Bill had had a very rough night, and the strong coffee was well... medicine. Both were stark naked wearing nothing but large hats, and were soaking wet after having just used the car-wash facilities to cool down. Bill looked just fine, the same as usual, Pedro on the other hand was an absolute mess. I thought it best to say nothing about yesterday… I knew that Pedro will tell me all about it later.

'Good morning boys it's a nice day I see your taking in some sunshine, got to keep-up your vitamin "D" level. Lesley and I thought that you guys might want to finish off this quiet weekend with a swim in our backyard pool and a bloody great steak-and-sausage bar-b-cue at our place tonight. We could finish off the night with two boring old 16mm movies, so what do you say chaps eh, cocktails at four is it?'

I detected an audible low groan from Pedro and observed a happy beaming smile and a thumbs-up sign from Bill.

Bill's depressed low had obviously turned around to a Bill high. I thought to myself, this must be how the "black dog" depression condition works. Well his high is going to be even higher and most likely very stiff when he finds-out what we have in store for him.

Our well-constructed plan was simple. We should keep Bill occupied and his mind off terminal things, however after last night's Bill-watch Pedro was now completely worn out. It was time for the next shift to take over, and I guess for now that would be Lesley and me.

At the same time, we had to come up with some cunning devious plan to get Bill and Mary together.... This was exciting stuff. I should have been an Indian matchmaker or something, maybe this could be the start of a new Multi Agencies business, a match-making service, then again time will tell.

As the old saying goes, "the success is in the baking and not in the making." It now appears that we had some very fine baking to do to get our required result.

Chapter: Seventeen.

Monsoon Entertainment

Life in a small-town is what you make-it. For every disadvantage, there was an even greater advantage, at least that's how I had always seen things in the remote North-West.

You have to remember, most of the permanent residents of Kununurra and the surrounding farming areas, had originally come from major cities and large agricultural areas around the world. We were a melting pot of many nationalities, living in what was then the most modern government built town in Australia.

The dry season population was around 4500 swelling to 6500 in the peak of the tourist season; however, now it was the wet season, so the population was well below 2000 because of the annual town migration south to avoid the hot monsoon season.

With a young average aged population of well-educated people, it's not long before somebody thinks up some magnificent way to entertain themselves. Road-drain and mud skiing was a popular past time for a while, until one of the American cotton farmers broke his arm and a leg.

This was exciting stuff to watch and take part in, mind-you conditions had to be just right.

There were no covered road drains, the storm water drains being large deep troughs alongside the road so you can imagine just how much water flowed down them in the wet season after a tropical downpour.

The Webber Plains road was a good road, as it had an exceptionally long, straight, and wide drain running almost its full length. Most people enjoyed the Ord Diversion Dam water sports like water-skiing and the like; however, in the wet season this was much too dangerous. Yes more dangerous than skiing on a roadside drain.

At this time of the year the mighty Ord River would be in full flood, ripping-up massive trees along the river banks by the roots, and throwing then headlong down the river. The trees would hit the concrete Diversion Dam's fifty-ton steel gates with such a force that you could hear the loud impact, and feel the shudder of the ground from the beer garden in the town pub, twelve kilometres away.

In this flood situation, the twenty massive gates would all be open, with the middle eight gates fully open to the forty-foot stops. Even in the open position, the water was still flowing at a high-level and at a very fast flow rate through the gap.

No this was not a time to consider water sports on the Ord River, and so what was a man to do with his idle water-skis, why not try a little irrigation channel, or road-drain, and mud skiing.

It was easy, just fix the ski-rope to your Ute's towbar, put-on your skis and away you go. Depending on how brave you were, or how intoxicated you or your trusted driver was, the speed was... well quite frankly the limit of vehicle. I have witnessed speeds in excess of one hundred and twenty kilometres an hour, yes very fast indeed... for a roadside storm drain.

Now the mud skiing bit was just as exciting. As the water, flowing in the road-drain dispersed, just as quickly as it appeared after a tropical downpour. This left a very nice base of slippery mud, first discovered by a drunken skier who had not noticed that all the water had... well drained away.

Kununurra mud is black very slimy-clay based stuff. The farmers think it is okay to grow things in and so do the people who sometimes get them-selves covered in it; however the stuff dries like bloody concrete.

Timing is the all important factor when using "Cununurra Clay," yes it even has its own special government invented name.

Unfortunately, if you should wait too long and the mud dries, then you're in big trouble getting the stuff off your skin; if you happen to hit a dry-spot while skiing at forty kilometres an hour, well you're in bigger trouble as the cotton farmer on that particular day found out.

Some forms of entertainment just sort-of create themselves. The opportunities are there but are never discovered until the penny drops, awakening the cunning inventive mind.

One day I was down at the pub listening to someone's disgruntled views about the lack of available local entertainment. At the time, there was no TV or radio within a thousand kilometres of Kununurra. The only radio was long-wave BBC and ABC with nothing exciting to listen to there. That only left canned music, long-play records, and music cassettes; also we had the town Picture Gardens, showing movies once a fortnight. We were in urgent need of some other form of entertainment.

One wet-season day while partaking of some male company and a drink at the Kununurra cave-bar, I clearly overheard a cranky station manager telling the uninterested barmaid about his stations only form of entertainment and that it had just broken-down.

The 16 mm projector was buggered, and he wasn't game to go back to the station without the bloody thing fixed. The only problem was, he couldn't find anybody in town to fix the damn thing. The barmaid, clearly disinterested in this topic suggested that he should talk to me as I fix electrical things.

It was more than obvious to me that this barmaid couldn't tell the difference between a light globe and a toaster. I proceeded to explain to the station manager that my company fix's radio communications equipment, RFDS radios and the like and we don't know a damn thing about 16mm projectors.

I might as well have been talking to the bar-top ashtray as the station manager continued on in detail as to what the projector problem was. I eventually conceded to having a look at his 16mm projector, so we both went over to my workshop to pull the thing to bits.

Less than half an hour later, I had managed to sort the problem out. Soon after we were both drinking rum and eating cheese and biscuits, while watching a test movie The Guns of Navarone.

The station manager was delighted, saying, 'Good on yer mate, yeh saved me bacon,' and then informed me that these projectors get a fair hammering out on the stations, mainly since the films were shown over and over again.

He advised that he had about three old broken-down projectors in the back shed… and then the idea hit-me. I suggested that he give me the old projectors, and any others he could get his hands-on from the other stations, my intention was to try and make a couple of good ones out of the lot.

"When your projector breaks down again, we will just exchange it for a loan one until I can get yours fixed.'

The idea went well and the message blasted out on the RFDS (Royal Flying Doctors Service) station chat session. I soon had about four 16mm projectors in good working order made up from about thirty old broken projectors sent in to me.

I soon discovered that film material was not a problem, as just about all the surrounding stations had movie hire accounts with 16 Millimetre Agencies drawing hire films out of Darwin and Perth.

Many movies each week were going through the Ansett airfreight terminal in Kununurra, going both up and return. I had arranged with the stations for all their returned movies dropped off at my Kununurra workshop office. I then held back for a day or two the ones that we wanted to see. In this way I now had endless amounts of free movie material to view.

With all this new movie material I had a brilliant idea and built a projector box (bio-box) into the wall of my office facing out into the mechanical workshop. We then built a large screen that could drop down when needed across the front workshop doors.

This was a great set-up since we then sat in the air-conditioned office and watched the movie through the large office windows. This was movie land bliss, especially with my well stocked built-in bar in the corner of my office, what more could a moviegoer want.

Well this was Kununurra, and they did want more.

They, my friends wanted to swim in my pool and have a bar-b-cue as well as watch a movie, so we did. I converted my house backyard into a small outdoor movie theatre. This was achieved with dual projectors mounted on the end of my concrete bar facing out into the backyard, where I had constructed a very large wide-angle cinemascope screen.

This was later to known as the "Dallas movie theatre," and became a very popular night out. One could cook a steak and have a swim or stand at the bar all while watching a free movie.

One very dark night while a John Wayne movie was on, I was engrossed in a particular exciting part. JW had just challenged the bloke in the black hat "It's your move, if yeah got the guts to draw?" then waiting in suspense for the baddy to draw…

Unknown to me, just then old Ben, an Aboriginal elder came quietly up behind me as I was standing at my bar; drink in hand poised and waiting for the answer. He tapped me on the shoulder while still deeply engrossed in the movie. When I turned around I almost pissed my pants with fright.

Old Ben, complete with his tribal marking scars; was not easy on the eye in the daytime, let alone in the dark of my backyard. He then very politely spoke to me.

'You bin mah friend long-time now ah ask you do some little thing for an ol man like me.'

I pulled myself together remembering this was a powerful and respected man in the Kimberley, replying with an involuntary squeaky voice.

'Anything Ben, what can I do for you Ben?'

'Could you bin just turn-up the fucking film-sound a bit mate, as ah can't hear dem film sounds like I used to when as was a young un?'

Ben then turned and looked the opposite way and I followed his gaze, and reeled back in astonishment. Across the road, the small mountain known as Mount Cyril was ablaze with pin points of torchlight, with many Aboriginal families. They had climbed high up the mountain slope to watch the movie over the top of my flat roofed house. Ben being the tribal elder, then asked by his people to approach me to have the sound turned up a bit, which of course I did.

These movie nights were quite exciting with many people enjoying the experience such as the local Police force. The hospital Doctors and nurses were regular attendees including the Pharmacist Keith who only lived two houses up the road.

A rather odd movie favourite cuisine was the Darwin fast-food order. If you put your mind to it nothing is impossible, only then can good magic easily performed almost on demand. All you need is some willing people who like a laugh, and will try just about anything, plus a jet-plane, a telephone, oh and a few dollars.

Kununurra never had a KFC (Kentucky Fried Chicken) or even a fish-and-chip shop, but Darwin did, about 900 kilometres away by road or one-hour by jet flight. First of all, you must invite the local Ansett airline boss and his family to a movie night. Then you get a friend in Darwin to place a fast food order for a hundred and fifty dollar worth of KFC, and a hundred dollar's worth of fish and chips all packed in a large insulated esky box, enough for forty guests.

Then you get the friendly airline boss to set-up a special Darwin to Kununurra direct priority freight pick-up, which then brings the food arriving piping hot to Kununurra in one hour.

We would then sit down to enjoy a movie eating Darwin fast food. We did this airfreight trick so many times; eventually the fast food shops in Darwin took our Kununurra phone orders direct to the aircraft. They thought this massive interstate food order extremely amusing and silly. It even caught the attention of the local newspaper The Northern Territory Times, who did a small story about the silly West Australians in Kununurra who had a passion for Darwin fast food.

Some movie nights were much more exciting than others, like the time when Doctor Dave Smith being called back to the hospital shortly after arriving with his family to enjoy some Darwin fast food and the movie.

The phone rang, it was for Doctor Dave, and he came dashing out of my lounge saying there was an emergency at the hospital. They couldn't reach the on duty Doctor, so he was it, and must go. Something about the Sergeant has had a suspected heart attack, and then he was gone in a flash.

His wife Anne remained, saying that they had been partying all afternoon, and this was Dave's first weekend off in the two months since arriving in Kununurra. The two police officers lying on sundeck chairs waiting for the movie to start shot-up on hearing this, as the only Sergeant they could think of was their boss.

The sad news soon got around the movie crowd, who had by then started to speculate on what may have happened to the Police Sergeant. The phone rang again, it was Doctor Dave. He would be back soon, and would explain everything when he arrived, could I please holdback starting the movie until he got there, and to pour him a large scotch and ice.

This message was quickly relayed to the movie crowd, and all agreed the medical emergency matter must have been a false alarm. We all waited in earnest to hear the full story on the Doc's return.

On his return Doc Dave explained that "The Sergeant" emergency was in fact one of the Aboriginal elders named "Sargent Maboo." Dave had seen Sargent (pronounced the same way as Sergeant) as a day surgery patient several times. He had advised him if he didn't give-up the drinking immediately, he would die as he had advanced cirrhosis of the liver.

Unfortunately, the elder was dead when the Doc arrived at the hospital, and there was nothing he could do for him. The man was a known alcoholic, he had died tonight of a massive liver failure. Doc Dave was grumbling on about the lack of any hospital staff around to help him get this very large man striped of his clothing, and into the freezer morgue.

Many people at the bar-b-cue movie knew "The Sergeant" (as he was known) quite well. As a mark of respect, we all drank a toast to the life of the Aboriginal elder and Sargent Maboo's passing.

We had around ten movies to choose from, as Monday was a holiday, all decided unanimously to have a marathon movie night. At about three-thirty in the morning, there was another phone call for Doc Dave who by this time was fast asleep on the back porch.

When he came back outside the Doc was furious cursing and ranting. The hospital had just advised him that the ALS (Aboriginal Legal Services) were not satisfied with diagnosis of the Aboriginal tribal elder Mr Sargent. The ALS had suggested that he had not received the proper medical help he should have, and were now disputing the cause of death. Doc Dave then found out that the ALS were also seeking an urgent independent autopsy carried out by the State Medical Examiner. They advised that the Medical Board would shortly serve Dave with a summons of compliance.

Dave was disgusted at this action, saying that he would sort this misunderstanding out in the morning. However, the question asked by all was why the hell was the ALS was getting involved with this elder's death, as they were in Kununurra on a completely different matter.

It was just bad luck I suppose that the ALS (Aboriginal Legal Service) were in town. They were actually in Kununurra to attend a Court hearing involving the local Hotel owner Frank Camer-Pesci, and two Aboriginal men caught red-handed stealing booze from Franks secure liquor warehouse.

It was in the early hours of the morning when Frank's limited sleep rudely interrupted. The cause being two Aboriginal men heard breaking into the Hotel's large liquor-storage shed to steal booze.

Frank caught the two men red handed in the act of stealing his booze. Both were then firmly tied-up with chains and secured with padlocks. Frank had a long chat with these two blokes and decided to make them stand out a bit by giving them both a haircut.

Frank, being an Italian, had always fancied himself as a hairdresser. He reckoned that if he had not been a successful hotelier, he would have most certainly considered the hairdressing business. The Mohawk style was all the rage at the time, so Frank proceeded to give them both the benefits of a free haircut, and his limited skills as a hairstylist.

The next morning Frank wrote out a note explaining that these two had broken into his liquor store last night. He then placed the note along with the padlock key into a brown envelope and sent the pair chained together along to the local Police station, complete with the brown envelope to give themselves up to the Police.

When these blokes gave themselves up at the Kununurra Police station, everything started to go wrong. Apparently, the Aboriginal booze thieves were immediately provided with a free taxpayer funded legal representation (which just happened to be our tax funded ALS)... then all hell broke loose. Frank was accused and later convicted of assault and false imprisonment. The court then imposed a fine on Frank for a total of six thousand dollars for catching these two thieves. The two Aboriginal plaintiffs being awarded by the court two thousand dollars each for being chained-up, (deprivation of liberty) and one thousand dollars each for the free haircut, the courts definition of (assault).

Frank has now decided that the hair styling business is not profitable. On a positive note, nobody has since that haircut event ever broken into the Kununurra Hotels liquor store, no doubt over the years saving Frank a great deal more than the six thousand dollars he paid out in fines.

As for me I suspect the main reason for avoiding Franks booze store was, if caught, the possibility of a bad haircut the offenders might receive.

Then Frank summed up the level of legal and court stupidity. Both these dumb Aboriginal thieves spent their awarded money at Franks Hotel buying booze... with Frank's money... crime does pay; these blokes even got a free haircut.

There was a hard thumping going on inside my head. I could feel the deep throbbing pain, something was happening in my head. Then some loud bells started ringing which caused me to enter into a further confused state.

The ringing was in phases of "two" then I thought I know that sound, then in realisation I woke-up, the phone just kept on ringing. I knew the only way it would stop was to answer the bloody thing.

'Hi I'm asleep, what the hell do you want at this time.' then glancing at the clock, 'it's a bloody holiday and it's only... what the hell, four thirty in the morning.'

I mentally stumbled and calculated that I had been asleep for only one hour.

'It's Doc Dave here. I need your help down at the hospital something's very important has just come up.'

Dave was talking much too fast for my brain, but it sounded like this was urgent, especially as he knew that I had been up all night watching movies and drinking... with him.

'I tell you what Dave, I'm just about to have something come-up myself, and I have one hell of a hangover. I think I might be dying.'

'Get your arse down here and quick. I will give you something to fix both problems, oh and make sure you come in through the back door of the Hospital. We don't want to wake-up the patients now do we?'

I hung-up the phone thinking what's this all about, and then sat upright. The pain was well beyond all previously known hangovers. Even if the Doc had not phoned, I think I would have been going down to the Hospital. This was bad but I had better hurry, something was going on that obviously needed my special skills.

Dave met me at the back door with a worried look on his face. He was also very cranky, motioning me with waving arms to hurry up.

'Quick follow me over to the morgue, I need a hand, take this,' handing me four different coloured pills and a plastic cup of water. 'And don't make a sound.'

The pills went down in one big gulp while I followed closely behind Doc Dave, down the dimly lit pathway.

I complained that the pills were not working but he completely ignored me, then Dave in a low voice started to tell me about the latest development on the "Sargent" story. Now I knew why Dave was so cranky.

The ALS had managed to convince the Medical Examiner that something was wrong with Doctor Dave's diagnosis, convincing them that the Aboriginal elder Sargent's cause of death may be wrong. Dave had been on the emergency phone-line to Perth, nevertheless the Medical Examiner's Office had decided to agree for the State Coroner's Office to send up a medical specialist to conduct a full autopsy on the elder Sargent...

The Coroner was arriving on the midday jet from Perth today, in only seven hours. I could tell that Dave needed some kind words of reassurance.

'Fuck, this sounds serious stuff Dave. You've got the ALS after you, and now you're own people, the Medical Board, is giving them their full support, oh and another thing if they do find anything wrong with this Aboriginal elders death you'll most probably get speared to death by the local tribe.'

Dave stopped so abruptly that I walked into him. My pounding head suffered a jolt that made me wince with pain. Dave turned to stare into my blood-shot eyes.

'What sort of a friend are you? I can assure you that all my dealings with this Sargent bloke were correct and professional. There is no error in my diagnosis, the man has a long documented medical record of advanced cirrhosis,' then he abruptly stopped his ranting. 'Why the fuck am I trying to justify my professional decisions and capabilities to a fuckwit like you?'

I looked down at my boots in shame realising that the Doc was obviously more than a little stressed-out about this autopsy matter. My light-hearted Kimberley humour was not going down too well at all. Dave turned away from me, in what I had thought disgust, then gripping the heavy metal handle threw open the door to the freezer morgue. I gasped aloud as I was suddenly hit in the chest by the blast of super cold air, then in my utter surprise.

'Jesus he's one hell-of-a big black bloke, is that the Sargent?' then another question came to mind. 'But why in the hell do you need any help from me, you know I'm not feeling very well?'

Dave turned to me and explained the situation as if he was talking to a little boy.

'First observation of the deceased should have brought to mind two important things, one is he's a bloody big heavy bloke, and the other is that he is frozen solid and stiff.'

Dave looked solemnly down at the Sergeant's naked frozen body then clasped his hands behind his back as if giving a medical lecture and continued.

'You will also no doubt notice that one arm and one leg have fallen off the stainless steel trolley, thus causing both limbs to splay out across the morgue.' Doc Dave spun on his heel turning to face me. 'Now, the immediate problem that should come into your dim mind is that now this big bugger won't fit into a standard bloody coffin; and the other... and might I emphasis this is the most important problem. Is that this body is required to be ready for an autopsy in approximately five and a half-hours time.

The Coroner will expect to find a fully thawed-out body, not one with arms and legs pointing in odd bloody directions.'

Then Doc Dave gave a small apologetic cough.

'I must have left the body holding straps off last night, in my haste, trying to get back to see the movie.'

I observed all these facts, and took in this important information into my throbbing hangover brain. Although I was still trying to figure out just why was I was standing in this freezer morgue at five in the morning when Dave spoke again.

'Quick give me a hand to get the Sargent outside and on to the back lawn. We'll leave him outside, and when the sun comes up he'll thaw-out faster.

With a bit of luck he might thaw-out enough to get his arm and leg back into the right place. If that ALS lot ever find him like this, they'll have my medical licence for sure.'

The first part of the move outside was easy as the trolley Sergeant was on, did have large wheels. Pushing and pulling we eventually got the Sergeant through the narrow morgue door on-to the pathway, then came the hard bit. This guy must have weighed over a hundred kilos, Dave and I started to man-handle him out on to the lawn area, and then Doc Dave yelled out... or maybe it was a scream.

'You stupid bastard if he falls off this bloody trolley he'll break a leg and maybe an arm and then I'll be right in the shit.'

I stopped pushing and shoving the heavy trolley, and with panting breath gasped out.

'What's the hell it matter Dave, this bloke's fucking dead he won't feel a thing.'

Dave screwed up his face in a contorted look of disbelief, and yelled into the ear of my sore head.

'His bleeding arm will snap off you idiot, he's still frozen rock-solid hard. Just what do you think the autopsy specialist would say if he were to be given a body to perform an autopsy on that was in six bloody bits?'

In anger, Doc Dave gave the stuck trolley a mighty shove and the thing tipped over onto the grass, spilling the Sergeant off the trolley with a mighty thud. Doc Dave gave out a loud high pitched ranting little girly scream.

'Oh my God... Shit, now look what you've done?'

I protested that it was he who pushed the trolley over, however as luck would have it the body was still in one piece, all was going to be okay now, or was it?

The noise must have woken-up the entire Hospital and all the surrounding houses. The lights and windows started to clatter open on all the nurse's quarters, female voices were demanding to know what the hell was going on, then came the unmistakable voice of the Hospital matron,

'Whose that in the morgue, is that you again Doctor Smith?'

Doc Dave froze as stiff as Mr Sargent was. He then stared at me with a terrified look on his face, bringing his finger to his lips in a gesture of silence. I thought how silly, he has woken the whole damn town up with his ranting and raving... Then again I remembered everybody was terrified of the little matron Bungi, a woman who ran this hospital with strict military precision, and an iron fist. She was the real boss of this Hospital… and Doc Dave knew it.

The last I had seen of the Sargent was he was lying on his side out on the back lawn of the nurse's quarters with one leg and one arm sticking up into the air. Doc Dave had gone to get a bed sheet to cover-up the Sargent's naked body and I was busy unconvincingly, trying to explain to three young nurses that had just arrived for duty that everything was all right and under Doctor David Smith's control.

Two days later Doc Dave came around to my office and we had a scotch to celebrate that the autopsy proved his diagnosis on the Sargent's death was correct. Nevertheless, it was a close thing, as Dave had only just managed to get the frozen limbs back into position prior to the autopsy.

About a week later, the town started filling up with hundreds of Aboriginals from all over the Kimberley. The Sergeant was sent off in true tribal style to meet his Aboriginal ancestors, with all due respect in a massive funeral befitting an elder of the local Aboriginal community.

Chapter: Eighteen.

Love finally found

The invite to the Sunday bar-b-cue movie at my place, was a well-designed cunning ploy to get Mary and Bill to meet. Or at the very least give Mary a chance to check out Bill.

Although we had a special love mission in mind, nobody attending would suspect this bar-b-cue movie night as anything other than normal, we now had quite regular movie nights. I had earlier discussed my suggested plan with Keith who thought it was a great idea, since he only lived two houses up the street. He and Mary could both walk over to my place and then he would stagger back alone, knowing a good deed done and mission complete.

My lovely wife Lesley thought that for this very special mission, we should try to keep the number of invited guests down to around fifteen or twenty-five people. In addition, we should also keep the purpose a secret. Only five people would know of this ultimate love plan, Pedro, Keith, Mary, Lesley, and me.

Morrie had made it clear that he felt bad about what had happened, and wanted a chance to apologise in person to Bill for his jealous outburst that had caused Bill to flip into this latest state of depression.

Morrie had heard on the Kununurra mumble vine that I might be having a bar-b-cue movie show tonight, thinking this might be the chance to resolve things. He was willing to give-up his usual Sunday night speedway meeting, to come along to set things right again, and to formally apologise to Bill.

I thought that this might be a great idea, two things resolved in one night, if we could only get the timing right, this could be a great event. Looking for further support I thought I might discuss this plan with Pedro. He was not happy about this plan when I rang him at home...

'How's the head going Pedro, you've had over six hours sleep. I reckon you and I need to discuss our Bill and Mary love plan. By the way I have just been talking to Morrie...'

A drowsy Pedro snapped back into life with a vengeance.

'You did what? Morrie is the bloke who started all this bleeding mess, he's a good mate of mine, but I don't think he's a mate of Bill's any more. Not after he accused Bill of screwing around with his wife Robyn.'

I thought hell what have I done wrong now, then jumping to my defence.

'Well that's just it Pedro; you see Morrie wants to set things right, starting with a full apology. Think about it Pedro; if we can get Morrie and Bill back as friends, that will set the stage for resolving Operation First Fuck. You know how Bill likes working on Morrie's speedway car, with that problem resolved first, it will open the way for... well for love. What do you think?'

I could almost hear the cogs grinding in Pedro's brain going over the possible advantages and probable disasters.

The risk was Bill might on first sight of Morrie just storm out and start working on another final solution. Bill is a strong man; it would take some extraordinary effort to stop him... or worse he might attack Morrie. One consolation came to mind, to my knowledge Bill has never been the cause of any violence. On the other hand I would guess there is always a first time.

Pedro; like me, had seen the large dents in the workshop metal doors and knew that a powerful punch from Bill in one of his tempers would be unforgettable... to whoever was on the receiving end. This could start a man with a nice easy-going nature, to travel down a future path of social destruction and memorable aggression. Pedro was silent and I was about to speak when he beat me to it.

'I think if we can make it work, that is, if we could get Bill and Morrie back together first. It could put Bill in the right frame of mind, once lubricated with a few rum and cokes, and full of steak-burger; he might just be ready for love. However, if we get it all wrong, we will be giving Mary a view of Bill's character that we have all never seen before. A side of him that we don't ever want to see, quite frankly it will fuckup any chances of completing Operation First Fuck.

Niven, I think we should play out our good hand of cards, and place our total trust in the Bill as the man that we know. He's basically a good bloke, a forgiver and not a bar-room fighter.'

I was almost in tears at those gallant rousing words by Pedro. With a sniffle I replied…

'I totally agree with you Pedro, we will give it our best try. I'll give Keith a call and tell him of the new variation to the love plan.'

There was a notable pause on the phone, and then Pedro cried out.

'Keith Wong, Jesus Christ, I hope he's not going to turn-up in that Caftan dress again. That will be the cause of an almighty bleeding fight for sure.'

I thought about that… Pedro was right. Cunning psychology was required in this very sensitive matter.

'I know Keith well, if there's one way to guarantee he "will" be wearing his Caftan, it would be to tell him not to wear it. Just the same as if you told him to arrive sober he would arrive drunk. Pedro, we have to accept that Keith is now a very important part of our plans to fix Bill's problem, and I know he really wants to see things turn-out okay, but I do hear you. If the bar-b-cue starts getting a little slow, then you can be sure to rely on Keith to liven things up a bit.'

Pedro shuffled the phone around and replied in a quiet voice.

'Then we will just have to make sure that Keith doesn't get bored and things don't slow down. I'll see you at around five o'clock, my headache pills should have worked by then.'

Next, I gave Keith a call and brought him up to date on the Morrie part of the plan. He was not keen on the idea of Morrie being at the bar-b-cue at all, especially as Morrie hadn't a clue about our detailed love plan for Bill.

'That Morrie bloke could stuff things up real good if Bill is still grumpy with him.' Keith the ever-direct man of action continued.

'We should concentrate our efforts on the main plan, to get Bill a fuck, not a bloody fight.'

Keith was right again; anyway, this conversation had now convinced me that Keith was as dedicated as Pedro and I were in helping Bill resolve his woman lust problem. We now had the means, firmly in our hands on how to fix up Bill's desires ... why take any risks. Yes, I could see his point of view but then again, how could Keith, a pharmacist fully understand Bill's other love, the love of motor cars. I attempted to explain this complicated situation to him.

'Let me try and explain Bill. His first love was probably his Mother, and then when he entered the workforce his first love was replaced by his love of motor cars. Now his priority in love is going to be the love of a woman. This means that the second most important thing on Bill's mind is his love of motor cars. Just think if we could resolve both of these enormous problems this very night... imagine what that would mean to Bill Gump?'

There was a distinct sound of a Jesus sigh. Keith had little patience for any distraction from the cause. He was a "no messing about" kind of person, straight to the point and no stuffing about. I was about to be educated on the art of direct thinking.

'Look, I know Bill's a nice kind of guy and all that, but we are talking about getting this virgin bloke his first real fuck. You keep on about Bill's so-called love of bloody cars; well as far as I have heard Bill has fucked-up more good cars than most blokes' have fucked a women.

If he maintains his current form, then he might start fucking up women just the same as his cars. He will need to change his depressive attitude, and soon. A crashed and lost motor car is nowhere near as bad as a lost woman to a man.'

Spot-on, Keith had hit the bullseye. There was much more to this matchmaking business than I or Pedro had first thought, and Keith was the living proof.

Only eight months earlier Keith had lost his beautiful wife in a terrible vehicle accident and it was painfully obvious to all that he was still grieving deeply over his loss. He may be a tough person; however, this was enough to bring anybody to their knees. The town of Kununurra was moved with deep understanding in the hope that time will help heal his pain.

Keith had a valid point though, that being if we got Bill started down the normal bloke path of a relationship with a woman, could it end-up the same as his cars... total wrecks? Then again, this was going to be a "once only" assisted sexual encounter... wasn't it?

'Keith we will need to time this event with military precision. I intend to get Bill over here early and explain that Morrie wants to apologise to him. When that suggestion is accepted, and I reckon it will. I will arrange for Morrie to arrive first to deliver his apology to Bill. Then if you and Mary can arrive shortly after this event you can introduce Mary to Bill, who by that time will be a happy man about making-up with Morrie... what do you think of the plan so far?'

'What time do you want us to arrive?'

'Oh I dunno, say about five thirty.'

There was a pause as Keith was putting some thoughts through his head on this important matter.

'It'll still be light then. I reckon Mary and I should get to your place after dark, say around six o'clock. Mary can check-out Bill in the twilight; this might be the best light in giving Bill some sort of a sporting chance. After all he's not the best looking bloke around is he?'

I thought, I wonder how Keith rates himself on the scale of good looks. Looks aren't everything are they? Bill may have some other female attraction. (Which we later found out he most certainly did have.)

'It sounds okay to me Keith, so let's go with that.'

The plan had to work just right to set the mood for Bill and Mary; nothing, but nothing must be left to chance. As they say in golf, we're looking for a hole in one here, not an Albatross, or a Birdie.

I was busy cleaning up the backyard from last week's party when I glanced at the clock and started to panic. It was close to five o'clock and there was still much to do. The sweat was dripping off me in the 40-degree plus heat. At least the temperature will drop by about seven degrees after dark.

Just then I heard a vehicle pull up and looked up to see that Bill had arrived, dressed correctly for courting in his old footy shorts and a dirty company t-shirt, finished off with well-worn rubber thongs displaying his dirty feet. He marched in the front gate with a big smile on his goatee-bearded face, which was odd for Bill. I must admit I was a little startled at this display of casual smiling attitude. After all, it was only some twenty hours ago he was trying to end his own life, and we were all out desperately looking for him before he could carry out a terminal act.

'Hi boss I thought I'd come over early and give you a hand in setting things up for tonight's movie.'

Bill was about the only person that I knew who would have considered that kind thought, and then he gently put down a large cardboard box on the bar and opened it to reveal a collection of good quality booze.

'I just wanted to thank all you blokes for thinking of me last night. I realise now that I have friends that care about me, so I've brought these few drinks along to say thanks.'

I was rummaging through this Aladdin's cave of bottles thinking good choice, two large bottles of rum, four bottles of nice red wine, and a bottle of black label scotch. I hardly noticed that Bill had started to talk again.

'I've decided to turn over a new leaf and stop being a miserable sod and start to smile a bit more, I'm going to try hard...'

There was a firm prod in my arm from Bill's stout finger,

'Are you listening to me boss?'

'Yes, yes, of course. If you could take those three bags of garbage out to the bins, then crank-up the bar-b-cue fire and clean it off. Then start cutting-up the meat that would be a great help to me Bill.'

Other people had just started to arrive, which meant that the bar needed to be in full functioning order first. The large ice-chest had to be filled-up with beer cans and submerged in the ice to achieve the expected maximum chilled effect.

All this distracted me from setting-up the dual projectors. On the other hand, it had also distracted me from telling Bill about the intended apology from Morrie, and that he was going to arrive here very soon... time ticked by. Too late, there erupted an almighty loud shouting argument over by the bar-b-cue. Morrie had slipped into the backyard from the boat-shed gate. I suddenly remembered Bill had not been primed about Morrie's intended apology. Bill's opening greeting was to say a bit hostile.

'What the fuck are you doing here you shithead bastard...'

It was not hard to guess that Bill had just caught sight of Morrie. I stopped my messing about at the bar and made my way briskly over to them, still holding two cans of chilled beer. As I approached, Bill had his back to me, and Morrie was looking at me over Bill's shoulder with a confused look. He had obviously thought I had told Bill of his proposed apology... he was wrong very wrong... my fault again.

When I arrived at the scene, the two were facing each other. Bill was furious, acting like a psycho madman.

His right-hand held a very large steak sandwich dripping with onions and tomato sauce, and his left hand held a very large butcher's knife with the tip resting on Morrie's chest. Everyone and everything fell silent; you could have heard a pin drop. Even the frogs had stopped croaking, and the last cricket had rubbed his legs just one more time to attract a mate and stopped to watch what was going to happen next.

The air was thick with tension. Everybody remained whisper-quiet, they all knew the story about Morrie accusing Bill of chatting-up his wife. This was a serious breach of a mate's trust, and a total disregard of the unwritten rule of the Kimberley. "Never covet another man's wife." I cleared my dry throat and in my best calm voice announced.

'Bill this is entirely my fault. I was supposed to tell you that Morrie wanted a chance to meet you face to face and have a few private words. Please, as a friend, you at least owe me this one small favour. Give Morrie a chance to say what's on his mind before you kill him.'

Nobody moved a muscle, the silence was deafening. I was trying to figure out just what was going on in Bill's mind. He would have to put down the sandwich, or the knife to pick-up his full rum and coke that was standing on the table next to him or... I guess he could park the knife in Morrie's chest first and achieve the same outcome. Without prompting Morrie quickly launched into his formal apology.

'Bill, all I want to say is that I'm really sorry about flying off the handle the other day, I was completely out of order. I guess I was jealous as Robyn was giving you far more attention than I was getting lately. I realise now that she was just feeling sorry for you, and I guess that's all there was to it.'

Bill's eyeballs started to bulge to what I thought was an impossible size. This was not a good sign. The knife went forward a fraction as Bill screamed out his loud response.

'Felt fucking sorry for me, you think Robyn felt bleeding sorry for me, you stuck-up conceited bastard. Why the hell would Robyn feel sorry for me eh?'

The knife again moved forward a fraction. Morrie's confident laid-back manner suddenly froze, his face turned white and his eyes opened wide in a look of utter terror. In stumbling words he continued, in an attempt to repair his awful apology to Bill.

'Bill, I only meant that Robyn was feeling sorry for you about me giving you shit all the bloody time, and, and... About me not appreciating all the help you've been with working on my speedway car. I've come here mainly to see you, and have even given-up going to tonight's speedway, especially to apologise to you. Robyn and me want you to come back out to the house again and forget all this crap, c'mon what do you say Bill?'

The look on Bill's face told me he was not at all convinced. In this forty-degree plus heat, Bill's temper was hotter. I had to do something quick to break the ice. I popped the top on one of the beer can's I was holding then turned and placed the other on the table next to Bill's rum, at the same time offering Morrie the beer and Bill his rum and coke. Morrie eagerly grabbed the ice-cold beer but Bill had no spare hand for his rum. The flittering pause of surprise was just enough for me to take the knife off Bill, and he then accepted his rum and coke. I nudged Bill with my elbow as a prompt for him to say something and he spoke in a low voice.

'Morrie, you're full of bull-shit, but I would still like you and Robyn to be my friends.'

The two old-new friends toasted drinks to the loud applause of the small but very relieved crowd of bar-b-cue movie onlookers. Bill then took a large bite out of his overloaded messy steak sandwich holding both arms in the air as a sign of acceptance like a winning boxer in the ring.

Just then there was a loud banging, it was Keith bashing my garden rake against my metal dustbin lid. Everybody turned to face the din.

'Ladies and gentlemen may I have your attention please,' there was a small delay as Keith waited for Bill's applause to settle down, which he thought was for him.

'Allow me to introduce to you all, my new Pharmacy assistant... Mary.'

Mary smiling took a small bow. She looked stunning in her latest city-style mini dress, her hair was perfect and her make-up, and stiletto heeled shoes finished off the perfect picture of a well-groomed good-looking woman.

A quick glance around my back-yard at the other women watching confirmed my suspicion. They were already working on a concentrated hate campaign, on the other hand, the men were wide-eyed gob-smacked like little schoolboys at this new female talent. I thought to myself oh dear, one problem resolved and another created. Just how would this special night turn out?

The crowd settled down to the normal conversation of complaining about the unbearable heat and the cost of trucked-in food from Perth, all the while drinking booze, and swimming in my pool. I walked over to Mary and Keith.

'Well hello there Mary remember me, might I say you look absolutely stunning tonight. Are you ready to meet the mechanical extraordinaire, the one, and only... Mister Bill Gump?'

Keith stumped me in my tracks. He could smell a potential shit disaster two latrines away and could sense the feel of recent tension in me.

'What the fuck's been going on over there at the bar-b-cue?'

'Oh that, don't worry, all fixed now. Bill and Morrie have decided to kiss and make-up over their bickering woman jealousy problem. They are back together again, everything's okay now.'

Keith reached for the bar behind him grabbing a drink for him and Mary who with furrowed and serious brow asked.

'Woman jealousy problem... Kiss and make-up... Back together again. I hope this is not the same Bill who you two want me to save?'

Keith gave me a look of detached pending disaster.

'You better explain that one Niven, we've just arrived' replied Keith dryly.

'It's all good news Mary. The very reason that Bill went into his depressive mood was that his friend Morrie got jealous when his wife Robyn was spending a bit of time with Bill trying to cheer him-up. It was all harmless stuff but Morrie accused Bill of trying to get into Robyn's pants. That was the jealousy part. Anyway, Morrie has just a minute ago apologised to Bill and now they are back as good friends. That was the kiss and make-up part... although those two blokes didn't actually kiss... if you know what I mean.'

Mary displayed a nice knowing smile and Keith looked relieved that I had come up with a decent story to explain all the cheering and clapping. I glanced across to the bar-b-cue noticing that Bill still with his back to us was in jovial discussion with Morrie, waving the meat tongs in the air for expression as he talked and turned the steaks and sausages on the hotplate. The thought occurred to me, Bill had not even noticed Mary when Keith did his intro thing? Now would be as good a time as any to introduce Mary to Bill.

'Come along Mary, you are now about to meet that special man in need.'

Mary took one step off the concrete hardstand in the dim light and gave a little yelp as her stiletto heels sunk deeply into my soft lawn. Her next step left her shoe firmly stuck in the grass, and both Keith and I lunged forward to save her from crashing into a row of chairs set-out for watching the movie. With a giggle Mary picked up her stilettos and placed them on the bar mumbling something about "that's off to a bad start." Mary now in bare feet followed me over to the bar-b-cue.

'Bill old chap, a moment of your valuable time please.' trying to gain Bill's attention from Morrie. 'Allow me to introduce to you the lovely Mary who has been waiting all this time to meet you.'

Bill turned around, and turned bright red with speechless embarrassment as he had just taken another large bite out of his messy steak sandwich. Mary extended her dainty hand in formal greeting. Bill quickly placed his sandwich on the table and wiped his greasy tomato sauce covered hand on his footy shorts, then grabbed Mary's hand in a powerful handshake. Mary gave out a small cry of pain signalling an immediate release to Mary's instant relief. With a face full of steak Bill mumbled.

'I am sorry I don't often get the chance to shake hands with a lady.' Then noticing how nice Mary was dressed, 'Had I known you were coming along I'd have worn something a bit better than this,' stepping back with arms wide showing his dirty t-shirt, footy shorts and thongs. Mary was quick to defuse the awkward moment.

'Maybe you could have worn your Caftan. I understand from my new boss that most of the guy's up here wear Caftans when they dress-up a bit.'

Bill looked puzzled, then realised that Mary was having a joke with him.

'You obviously work for the Pharmacist Keith. He's the only bloke around here that's game enough to wear a bloody Caftan in public. I get enough smart-arsed comments down the pub as it is, without giving those bastards there any more excuses,' suddenly halting his defence in mid-sentence. 'Oh please excuse my unforgivable swearing.'

Mary laughed aloud and asked for a paper towel to wipe the tomato sauce off her hands, which by a stroke of luck Bill managed to find very easily. Bill was performing at his awkward best, everything he said sounded like bumbling rubbish. I had my suspicion that Bill was rather besotted with Mary... some magic was obviously working. A pleasant thought occurred to me that this might just turn out all right. Playing cupid was good fun, but I must leave these two, as there was still much bar-b-cue work to do.

Someone standing next to me started to grumble about when would the movie start as his wife and kids were getting cranky. I used this as a good excuse to leave Bill and Mary chatting away together, and headed back to the bar and the projectors. Pedro and Keith were there huddled together in serious conversation, as I approached they both abruptly stopped; then stared at me with the innocence of two little boys who have yet to admit breaking the front window.

'What's going on, you two are holding out on me. I can both smell a rat, and tell that something's up?'

Pedro hunched his shoulders, a sign telling me that he was somehow going to try and reduce the shock. Keith looked on in silence with a wise and knowing look on his face.

'We've just been thinking it looks like we might have finally resolved "Operation First Fuck." Our good-mate deed will have been completed, but have you blokes thought about the consequences of what might happen afterwards.'

Pedro paused for effect giving me time to take-in what he was saying.

'I mean, just think. Bill will have had his first screwing experienced and have satisfied all the natural instincts of a lustful man,' then raising his finger to his eye-level in a scholarly salute.

'But this may-well be his only bleeding experience. After a few days of screwing bliss, what sort of whacko depression do you think Bill might descend into? We might have solved one problem and caused another, a far worse problem... that of knowing just what he is actually missing out on.'

Keith flashed one of his evil grins and remarked dryly.

'Well at least the bastard will have topped himself knowing what a good fuck was all about. Anyway, I don't agree with you Pedro, it's a man's natural instinct to find more pussy after the first plunge and not call it a day, or giving up the chase. I reckon he'll be okay. After all, the chase is the best part isn't it?

'

I must admit the thought of what may happen after completing our mission had never occurred to me. Now completed, we were presented with two differing views on how Bill might react, or handle this almighty new sexual experience. Still I had to admit both views had some merit, then again, it was all too late now. Raising my glass in a toast, all three of us with left-hand on our hips clinked our glasses like the three Musketeers, in self-congratulation of a job well done. Sipping my drink, I launched into a new strategy.

'I think that we have all done a bloody good job to date, and by the looks of things over there, you never know, after the deed Mary might get interested in Bill. We should work on keeping the interest going and set-up a date. What about us organising a dinner date for them both tomorrow night at Gulliver's Tavern?'

Pedro didn't so look sure; how would we persuade Mary to go out with Bill at such short notice. Keith had the firm view that Bill should sort out his own love life from now on.

'We've done more than most blokes would do for a friend.'

He then said in his best Councillor bureaucratic voice.

'Friends, Bill is now on the true path, treading the water in expectation, thrown into the deep-end of the pool of life. From now on he should learn to swim or sink, just like the rest of us blokes.'

This swim or sink thing was later to become an accurate reality.

I flicked on the projector and an old John Wayne cowboy movie cranked into life the guests then settled down to eat, drink and fall asleep in that order.

Old projectors require constant tweaking to keep them going correctly and that was what I was attending to when this almighty commotion started. The noise was in the darkness, just out of the glow of the projector light. I caught a glimpse of arms and legs tumbling in the air, together with loud cursing, followed by a massive splash. I had witnessed a dim vision of Bill Gump being unceremoniously thrown into my above-ground swimming pool by Pedro and Keith.

Keith started telling Bill in a very loud voice that it was a disgrace for him to come to a family bar-b-cue dressed in his dirty work clothes. Bill was spluttering in the pool trying to defend himself, at the same time trying to stay above water yelling that he didn't know that he was going to meet a nice lady. The other women on hearing that started throwing beer cans at Bill. I could see this bar-b-cue night was shortly going to turn into a riot, I yelled out.

'Hey you bastards that pool cost me a lot of money to keep clean. You've just chucked Bill in with all his bloody dirty work-clothes into my nice clean pool.'

Bill was shrieking like a little girl, everybody had forgot that Bill couldn't swim and Bill never thought to just simply put his foot down on the bottom and stand up in the shallow one and a half metre deep pool. Pedro was trying to grab Bill and save him from drowning while Keith was busy carrying out the process of removing all of Bill's dirty work clothes, and succeeded. Twenty seconds later Bill leapt out of the pool, just as I had decided to end this rude disruption, stopping the projector and switching on my powerful backyard floodlights.

A strange long silence followed... Bill stood there wide-eyed like a rabbit caught in a spotlight, stark bollock naked. Just then a firm voice made an observing comment from the crowd, which just happened to be one of the local coppers.

'For fucks sake Bill stab anyone with that and I'd have to take you in for assault with a deadly weapon.'

There followed much laughter and shuffling of the women moving in to get a better viewing position for a gander at Bill's equipment... Bill was not amused and turned bright red in embarrassment trying to cover his large unused tool with his hands. Just then, I felt a light tap on my shoulder, it was a smiling Mary.

'Can I borrow a towel for Bill? He seems a little upset about all this boy playacting stuff. You guys certainly have some fun. I think if the girls will eventually accept me, then I'm really going to like it up here in Kununurra.'

I got Mary a big bath towel and she was halfway over to Bill when Keith lent forward and whispered to Mary loud enough for all to hear. Why don't you make sure Bill gets home okay? I think we may have taken our fun a bit too far tonight. The crowd all Cooooed a loud sigh, and I distinctly heard a lone female voice say 'lucky bastard' as Mary rushed Bill out like a naughty child to one of my hire vehicles that he was using.

The next morning I was in my office going through the banking accounts, trying to work out which of the lucky bastards who had supplied me goods last month was going to get paid. Suddenly the office door burst open, Pedro came in clutching two mugs of steaming hot coffee. He looked like shit, and his eyes were like black holes.

'What's up with you bro-in-law you look like you didn't get any sleep last night.'

Pedro slumped down into a chair and glumly told me his sad story.

'We're going to have to shift either my caravan or Bills caravan, when I got home last night his little caravan was rocking on its axles as he was giving Mary one. The noise was hard to ignore and I was happy for Bill. I mean this was absolute and concrete evidence that Operation First Fuck was a total and roaring success.'

'So why the glum face Pedro. Do you realise that we have just saved a man's life,' then in my lifting compassionate expression, 'Do you also realise that this is a whole new beginning for our good friend Bill Gump. This may have set him on a new path to experience a beautiful life. We have all done well my friend...'

Just then I was rudely interrupted by Pedro, who had quickly lifted his hand in a signalling motion; instantly calling for immediate silence to my raving. I politely waited for his comment before proceeding; however, this never happened. Instead, Pedro lifted one cheek of his arse off the chair and let go a well manufactured fart which echoed throughout my serine office... obviously Pedro was not impressed by my glowing version of the possible Bill Gump events. Then as if nothing had happened, he continued his story.

'At ten thirty when I got home last night I said he was giving her one well that's not quite right because he gave her two, then three, then four, five, and six. I tell you what; I'll bet you he's bloody-well giving her one right now.'

I looked into Pedro's distressed face and recognised a genuine low, a look of total physical exhaustion. Now I knew the reason for Pedro's tired look, that's why the poor bastard never got any sleep last night. However, I did have my doubts; nobody could root for that long and survive. Nevertheless, I must confess, it was an interesting thought... was Bill still screwing Mary. I glanced at my watch, it was after all seven thirty. Let me see that would make it over nine hours of continuous screwing... impossible.

I don't know why, but we both crept down stairs from my office. The outer office staff stopped what they were doing for a moment and thought we were both going mad. We then peeked around the workshop door. Yes Bill's caravan was rocking madly from side to side he was still at it; Pedro looking on announced.

'There you go, I told you so... the bleeding fuckers have been fucking all bleeding night. It's a wonder they haven't caused each other some sort of grievous fucking bodily injury.'

I was trying hard to dissemble Pedro's normal every day swearing words, from the normal descriptive swearing words, to make a sensible sentence out of what Pedro had just said when I realised what time it was. I briskly walked across to Bill's caravan and bashed hard on the side. All of a sudden the rocking and the groaning stopped, then a weak but clearly audible Bill voice said,

'Yes... who is it?'

'It's me you bastard, your late for bloody work it's seven thirty, we've got a workshop full of broken Toyota's to fix today, I hope you're up to it.'

Pedro looked at me with a knowing grin then I realised what I had just said,

'Forget about the "up-to-it" bit and just get your arse, and everything that's attached to it out here. There were a few girlie giggles in the caravan and we left them to it again.

Bill and Mary soon became an item. That night Bill took Mary to Gulliver's Tavern for a magnificent dinner and worked hard (excuse the pun) on being the perfect courting gentleman. I think this relationship started out as one of lust and became one of love; however, it was not without its odd dramas.

About two months later Bill had decided to take Mary out on a picnic to a beautiful place called Black Rock Falls. This place is only some forty kilometres from Kununurra, unfortunately this nice picnic came with problems that nearly ended up in disaster. From my viewpoint, a number of unfortunate happenings continued to plague Bills life, following him, even into love. Apparently Bill and Mary had enjoyed a nice day out at Black Rock, and then as darkness fell, they both decided to have a skinny dip in the beautiful rock pool. Bill being a thoughtful gentleman had turned on the headlights of the company workshop Ute to light-up the dark rock pool. By nine o'clock and time to go home, Bill discovered that the battery on the Ute was now so low it could not crank over to start-up the big V8 engine. Being an automatic, and parked towards the pool on a steep slopping gravel road, they had no chance of push-starting the Holden Ute. They were well and truly stuck.

Bill remembered that the Ute had a CB radio and attempted to call someone at the office. Being a Sunday night and some twenty kilometres outside the normal direct line-of-sight working range of this radio, the call proved a useless effort. By around two in the morning Bill had noticed a number of people were heard quite clearly talking on his CB radio. He was not aware of the "skip" phenomenon of this type of 27 MHz CB radio but after a few tries he did managed to talk to some CB radio guy in Canberra... yes Canberra, 3000 kilometres away.

This same guy then called the Canberra Federal Police, who then contacted the WA State Police, who in turn phoned the local Police in Kununurra, upping the story along the way from a simple flat battery problem to an urgent SOS call. The local Police were then required to carry out a full search and rescue to find Bill and Mary.

The local Cops knew of Bill Gump and whom he worked for, they then rang my office, no doubt to collect evidence that may help them in this big rescue mission. By this time all were convinced that this was some sort of a hoax.

I was out flying when I got a company radio call at about 6:30am it was a frantic Pedro on the company air-band radio. He let go with a furious torrent of jumbled words.

'He's still at it, Bill's fucked-up again. This time he has the Federal State Police, and local cops on to him over some hoax radio call last night now he has started a bleeding Kimberley manhunt... looking for Bill.'

Manhunt what the hell, this can't be right we've fixed up all Bills problems. He's a normal guy now; everything should be okay with him.

'Hold on their Pedro there's got to be some simple explanation,' then it came to me. Bill had asked me for the loan of the workshop Ute to take Mary out to Black Rock Falls. 'I bet you that Bill and Mary are still at Black Rock Falls, he borrowed the Ute yesterday. The idea was to go there for a swim and a picnic. I'm not far from Black Rock; I'll fly over that way right now.'

Sure enough, Bill was standing on the back of the workshop Ute, waving his arms like a mad windmill with Mary standing alongside in her bikini. I reported my find back to Pedro. The Local Police then informed that Bill and Mary were okay, and that it was most likely just a simple vehicle breakdown. Pedro told the local Police he would go and sort the problem out. He then headed out to Black Rock Falls and started up Bill's Ute with some simple battery jumper cables... a two minute job.

The next day all the Australian national newspapers had the story as the inside cover news.

The Daily News, and the West Australian, and many others ran the story. A half page of a "Pag" cartoon sketch on the incident printed on the 13th October 1977. It portrayed Sir Charles Court talking into a microphone in front of a large CB radio with his cabinet ministers standing around him, the caption said; "I thought Canberra might listen to me and help us if we got in touch by CB radio." Apparently at the time Sir Charles was having great difficulty communicating and obtaining Canberra Federal funding for his various Western Australia State Government projects.

This unusual incident had caught the public interest, Bill and Mary were now famous media stars, and much sought after for radio and newspaper interviews.

Shortly after this event, Mary left Kununurra to settle matters regarding her divorce in Perth, the lovesick Bill soon followed her down to Perth. They married a few months after Marys divorce had become final, and then continued living a happy life together in Perth Western Australia for over thirty years. Sadly, Mary died of breast cancer in 2008.

Sadly, Bill never knew that Mary had terminal breast cancer until the last few weeks of her life. This sad situation was carefully planned, as the family did not want Bill to know of this pending tragedy, thus protecting his loss and love of Mary to the very end.

----THE END ----

CALL FOR CB 'MAYDAY' BAND

Channel 9 on Citizens' Band radio should be reserved as an emergency frequency, a man who was rescued from his broken-down car near Kununurra said today.

Mr Bill ███ (25), of Kununurra, said he and a friend spent 12 hours without food or water until their CB distress signal was heard 3000km away in Canberra.

"We went out to Black Rock—about 40km from Kununurra—for a picnic barbecue. About 4 o'clock we decided to go home and found the ute had a flat battery," he said.

"Being a mechanic, I tinkered around with it, but it was no good. We heaved it back up the slope about 10 metres but it wouldn't start.

"I was calling on the CB at odd times but I couldn't raise anybody locally.

"The next morning I raised a man in Sydney. He told me to try channel 9 because a group in Canberra man that channel 24 hours a day, listening for emergency calls.

"The woman in Canberra called up Perth. They called Kununurra police and about an hour and a half later they turned up and found us," he said.

He said the Federal Government should officially reserve channel 9 for emergency calls.

"A lot of us CB operators stay off channel 9, anyhow, to leave it clear for emergencies, but it would help to have it official," he said.

His distress call had probably reached Canberra by the skipping effect of the signal,

P&G Cartoon 13th Oct 1977

'I thought Canberra might help us too if we got in touch by CB radio.'

Introduction: About the Author

I was born in Edinburgh Scotland, this making me a true Scotsman with the full rights to wear the tartan... the Dallas Clan tartan.

My working background covers a number of trades and disciplines, with many years based in the north west of Australia. There I worked, owned, and operated; as the founder of a number of small, but varying types of business ventures. These ventures included a long career in RF communication systems, mining claim pegging, contracting to the mining industry, electrical and musical retail, aviation air charter, vehicle hire, and automotive sales and service.

After twenty odd years of ten hour days, and seven day working weeks. The family and I moved down to Perth Western Australia. There becoming a director/owner of yet another radio-systems sales and service company, "Communications Australia Pty Ltd." This new venture was promptly followed by a classic and vintage vehicles sales business. "The Toyshop." Then for some unknown reason, I drifted into the herbs and spice wholesale business, "Whittington's," and then into owning a Mexican restaurant "Zapata's."... Why, I really don't know.

I remain as planned happily married with beautiful children, who have now given us beautiful grandchildren.

My hands-on diverse business background has provided me with a long list of interesting true-life experiences to write this, and other novels.

I am fortunate in having a wide range of odd life experiences. They go, well together with my sound technical input, and a wild and cynical imagination. This combination also offers me endless material to write another genre I have called. Convincing, modern, realistic fiction.

For those that are interested, yes, Dallas is a real Scottish name. Moreover, there is indeed a Dallas tartan, and there is also a Dallas Scottish clan. Would you believe, also a town of Dallas near Forres in Scotland, including an ancient crest (the family coat-of-arms)

There is also a Niven Scottish clan, and crest; but not so flash or having as much fame… Unless you count "David Niven" the well-known actor as a credit, being the author of, "The Moons a Balloon" and "Bring on the Empty Horses."

Strange as it may be, remembering the many odd things in my life that just sort-of happened to be, you can't beat having your family name being part of a real ancient town in Scotland. We cannot finish without the mention of the famous city of Dallas in America.

Well yes that's odd too. You see George Mifflin Dallas 1759-1864 was Vice-President of America, to the 11th President James K. Polk, and gave his name to the now famous city of Dallas in Texas. This gentleman's great, great, great-grandfather was born in the town of Dallas Scotland having a direct lineage to Sir William de Ripley 1165 given lands on Dallas Scotland by King William the Lion.

Interesting, do you not think?

9 7 8 0 9 8 7 5 8 3 3 3 8